# Managing Schools

Patrick Whitaker

the Institute
of Management

*F O U N D A T I O N*

BUTTERWORTH
HEINEMANN

Butterworth-Heinemann
Linacre House, Jordan Hill, Oxford OX2 8DP
A division of Reed Educational and Professional Publishing Ltd

℞ A member of the Reed Elsevier plc group

OXFORD   BOSTON   JOHANNESBURG
MELBOURNE   NEW DELHI   SINGAPORE

First published 1998

**British Library Cataloguing in Publication Data**
A catalogue record for this book is available from the British Library

ISBN 0 7506 2194 X

Composition by Genesis Typesetting, Rochester, Kent
Printed and bound in Great Britain by
Biddles Ltd, Guildford and King's Lynn

# Contents

# Series adviser's preface

This book is one of a series designed for people wanting to develop their capabilities as managers. You might think that there isn't anything very new in that. In one way you would be right. The fact that very many people want to learn to become better managers is not new, and for many years a wide range of approaches to such learning and development has been available. These have included courses leading to formal qualifications, organizationally-based management development programmes and a whole variety of self-study materials. A copious literature, extending from academic textbooks to sometimes idiosyncratic prescriptions from successful managers and consultants, has existed to aid – or perhaps confuse – the potential seeker after managerial truth and enlightenment.

So what is new about this series? In fact, a great deal – marking in some ways a revolution in our thinking both about the art of managing and also the process of developing managers.

Where did it all begin? Like most revolutions, although there may be a single, identifiable act that precipitated the uprising, the roots of discontent are many and long-established. The debate about the performance of British managers, the way managers are educated and trained, and the extent to which shortcomings in both these areas have contributed to our economic decline, has been running for several decades.

Until recently, this debate had been marked by periods of frenetic activity – stimulated by some report or enquiry and perhaps ending in some new initiatives or policy changes – followed by relatively long periods of comparative calm. But the underlying causes for concern persisted. Basically, the majority of managers in the UK appeared to have little or no training for their role, certainly far less than their counterparts in our major competitor nations. And there was concern about the nature, style and appropriateness of the management education and training that was available.

The catalyst for this latest revolution came in late 1986 and early 1987, when three major reports reopened the whole issue. The 1987 reports were *The Making of British Managers* by John Constable and Roger McCormick, carried out for the British Institute of Management and the CBI, and *The Making of Managers* by Charles Handy, carried out for the (then) Manpower Services Commission, National Economic Development Office and British Institute of Management. The 1986 report, which often receives less recognition than it deserves as a key contribution to the recent changes, was *Management Training: context and process* by Iain Mangham and Mick Silver, carried out for the Economic and Social Research Council and the Department of Trade and Industry.

It is not the place to review in detail what the reports said. Indeed, they and their consequences are discussed in several places in this series of books. But essentially they confirmed that:

- British managers were undertrained by comparison with their counterparts internationally.
- The majority of employers invested far too little in training and developing their managers.
- Many employers found it difficult to specify with any degree of detail just what it was that they required successful managers to be able to do.

The Constable/McCormick and Handy reports advanced various recommendations for addressing these problems, involving an expansion of management education and development, a reformed structure of qualifications and a commitment from employers to a code of practice for management development. While this analysis was not new, and had echoes of much that had been said in earlier debates, this time a few leading individuals determined that the response should be both radical and permanent. The response was coordinated by the newly-established Council for Management Education and Development (now the National Forum for Management Education and Development (NFMED)) under the energetic and visionary leadership of Bob (now Sir Bob) Reid, formerly of Shell UK and the British Railways Board.

Under the umbrella of NFMED a series of employer-led working parties tackled the problem of defining what it was that managers should be able to do, and how this differed for people at different levels in their organizations; how this satisfactory ability to perform might be verified; and how an appropriate structure of management qualifications could be put in place. This work drew upon the methods used to specify vocational standards in industry and commerce, and led to the development and introduction of competence-based management standards and qualifications. In this context, competence is defined as the ability to perform the activities within an occupation or function to the standards expected in employment.

It is this competence-based approach that is new in our thinking about the manager's capabilities. It is also what is new about this series of books, in that they are designed to support both this new structure of management standards, and of development activities based on it. The series was originally commissioned to support the Institute of Management's Certificate and Diploma qualifications, which were one of the first to be based on the new standards. However, these books are equally appropriate to any university, college or indeed company course leading to a certificate in management or diploma in management studies.

The standards were specified through an extensive process of consultation with a large number of managers in organizations of many different types and sizes. They are therefore employment based and employer-supported. And they fill the gap that Mangham and Silver identified – now we do have a language to describe what it is employers want their managers to be able to do – at least in part.

If you are engaged in any form of management development leading to a certificate or diploma qualification conforming to the national management standards, then you are probably already familiar with most of the key ideas on which the standards are based. To achieve their key purpose, which is defined as achieving the organization's objectives and continuously improving its performance, managers need to perform four key roles: managing operations, managing finance, managing people and managing information. Each of these key roles has a sub-structure of units and elements, each with associated performance and assessment criteria.

The reason for the qualification 'in part' is that organizations are different, and jobs within them are different. Thus the generic management standards probably do not cover all the management competencies that you may need to possess in your job. There are almost certainly additional things, specific to your own situation in your own organization, that you need to be able to do. The standards are necessary, but almost certainly not sufficient. Only you, in discussion with your boss, will be able to decide what other capabilities you need to possess. But the standards are a place to start, a basis on which to build. Once you have demonstrated your proficiency against the standards, it will stand you in good stead as you progress through your organization, or change jobs.

So how do the new standards change the process by which you develop yourself as a manager? They change the process of development, or of gaining a management qualification, quite a lot. It is no longer a question of acquiring information and facts, perhaps by being 'taught' in some classroom environment, and then being tested to see what you can recall. It involves demonstrating, in a quite specific way, that you can do certain things to a particular standard of performance. And because of this, it puts a much greater onus on you to manage your own development, to decide how you can demonstrate any particular competence, what evidence you need to present, and how you can collect it. Of course, there will always be people to advise and guide you in this, if you need help.

But there is another dimension, and it is to this that this series of books is addressed. While the standards stress ability to perform, they do not ignore the traditional knowledge base that has been associated with management studies. Rather, they set this in a different context.

The standards are supported by 'underpinning knowledge and understanding' which has three components:

- Purpose and context, which is knowledge and understanding of the manager's objectives, and of the relevant organizational and environmental influences, opportunities and values.
- Principles and methods, which is knowledge and understanding of the theories, models, principles, methods and techniques that provide the basis of competent managerial performance.
- Data, which is knowledge and understanding of specific facts likely to be important to meeting the standards.

Possession of the relevant knowledge and understanding underpinning the standards is needed to support competent managerial performance as specified in the standards. It also has an important role in supporting the transferability of management capabilities. It helps to ensure that you have done more than learned 'the way we do things around here' in your own organization. It indicates a recognition of the wider things which underpin competence, and that you will be able to change jobs or organizations and still be able to perform effectively.

These books cover the knowledge and understanding underpinning the management standards, most specifically in the category of principles and methods. But their coverage is not limited to the minimum required by the standards, and extends in both depth and breadth in many areas. The authors have tried to approach these underlying principles and methods in a practical way. They use many short cases and examples which we hope will demonstrate how, in practice, the principles and methods, and knowledge of purpose and context plus data, support the ability to perform as required by the management standards. In particular we hope that this type of presentation will enable you to identify and learn from similar examples in your own managerial work.

You will already have noticed that one consequence of this new focus on the standards is that the traditional 'functional' packages of knowledge and theory do not appear. The standard textbook titles such as 'quantitative methods', 'production management', 'organizational behaviour' etc. disappear. Instead, principles and methods have been collected together in clusters that more closely match the key roles within the standards. You will also find a small degree of overlap in some of the volumes, because some principles and methods support several of the individual units within the standards. We hope you will find this useful reinforcement.

Having described the positive aspects of standards-based management development, it would be wrong to finish without a few cautionary remarks. The developments described above may seem simple, logical and uncontroversial. It did not always seem that way in the years of work which led up to the introduction of the standards. To revert to the revolution analogy, the process has been marked by ideological conflict and battles over sovereignty and territory. It has sometimes been unclear which side various parties are on – and indeed how many sides there are! The revolution, if well advanced, is not at an end. Guerrilla warfare continues in parts of the territory.

Perhaps the best way of describing this is to say that, while competence-based standards are widely recognized as at least a major part of the answer to improving managerial performance, they are not the whole answer. There is still some debate about the way competencies are defined, and whether those in the standards are the most appropriate on which to base assessment of managerial performance. There are other models of management competencies than those in the standards.

There is also a danger in separating management performance into a set of discrete components. The whole is, and needs to be, more than the sum of the parts. Just like bowling an off-break in cricket, practising a golf swing or forehand drive in tennis, you have to combine all the separate movements into a smooth, flowing action. How you combine the competencies, and build on them, will mark your own individual style as a manager.

We should also be careful not to see the standards as set in stone. They determine what today's managers need to be able to do. As the arena in which managers operate changes, then so will the standards. The lesson for all of us as managers is that we need to go on learning and developing, acquiring new skills or refining existing ones. Obtaining your certificate or diploma is like passing a mile post, not crossing the finishing line.

All the changes and developments of recent years have brought management qualifications, and the processes by which they are gained, much closer to your job as a manager. We hope these books support this process by providing bridges between your own experience and the underlying principles and methods which will help you to demonstrate your competence. Already, there is a lot of evidence that managers enjoy the challenge of demonstrating competence, and find immediate benefits in their jobs from the programmes based on these new-style qualifications. We hope you do too. Good luck in your career development.

*Paul Jervis*

# Preface

This book is about schools and those who work in them. It explores the complex challenges facing the education service as we move into a new century and a new millennium, and considers the ways in which schools will need to adapt to faster change in the years ahead.

I have long been fascinated with a view often put forward by those who work in industrial and commercial organizations, that schools do not need managing and that teachers are not part of the real world. Organizing a classroom of children and teaching subjects, the argument goes, is not the same as the hard-edged world of productivity, profitability, market share and customer needs. This is true. Schools are concerned with quite different things, many of which are as difficult to manage as those in business enterprises.

Bringing about continuous change in the hearts and minds of children and young people is a daunting task. Attempting to do this with only one person in mind is difficult enough, to do it for thirty or so others at the same time seems a preposterous idea. The product schools are concerned with is change itself – a largely invisible, inaudible and intangible commodity. While we strive to standardize our outputs, we know that individuality will largely defy it. The profits schools attempt to build are also extremely difficult to calculate – the gains made by each pupil each day in knowledge, understanding, insight, skill, capability, confidence and enterprise. Because schools are not involved in the same world of products, competition and markets as other types of organization it does not mean that they are not part of the real world, it is that their realities are different, often more elusive, more abstract and more volatile.

Educational management has only become a discrete discipline during the last twenty-five years or so. While ideas and models from the industrial and commercial world do have some relevance, these have not always transferred comfortably into schools. The focus of educational management has been on the senior positions in schools, particularly on heads and deputies. This is to assume that it is the institution that has to be managed, and not the central process it is concerned with.

In this book I work from the assumption that it is learning that has to be managed. This means, of course, that management and leadership is a function of all staff. I find it surprising that teacher training has not adopted a more significant management focus in its curriculum. Traditionally listed management functions – creativity, planning, organizing, communicating, motivating, co-ordinating and evaluating – are at the very heart of what teachers do in their professional work, but we have tended to leave the teaching part out when we talk about the management of schools.

Among the many fascinating features of schools are the different layers and levels of management. There is strategic management, conducted these days alongside governors; there is subject management, through departments in secondary schools and through co-ordinators in primary schools; there is the management of the curriculum and how it will be structured; there is the management of learning, a continuous series of interactions between teachers and their pupils; and there is the management of classroom life, the creating of a climate conducive to effective learning.

I have never held the view that management is a simple process, despite the seductive appeal of books, bandwagons and gurus. There are no straightforward and easy ways to do it, no simple solutions and no quick fixes. Management work is full of uncertainties, confusions, obstacles and ambiguities, and in schools we face a constantly changing cluster of cognitive muddles, intellectual paradoxes and personal dilemmas. Those who work in schools are faced with some of the most daunting and demanding challenges devised by society.

What I love about management so much is its intrinsic developmental quality. We can never truly say that we can do it, that we have arrived at optimum competence and we know how it works. Whatever our role or status in the scheme of things, we have a job with infinite possibilities, unpredictable situations and indeterminate solutions. Perhaps our only hope is to see the job as a development project in which we learn deliberately and continuously by every means at our disposal, and it is in this spirit that the book is offered.

Essentially it is a book about behaviour and the factors that affect it. In particular it emphasizes the importance of how we think and feel, what we say and do and how we learn from these experiences. Each chapter takes a key aspect of management and delves into it in search of meaning and significance. The theories and propositions are put forward not because they are right or true, but in order to stimulate thinking and enquiry. While management is intensely practical, conducted through countless interactions during the school day, it is a business of complex ideas, intricate systems and turbulent processes.

I hope those who read the book will find it a helpful mirror to their own experience, and will use the reflective activities within each chapter as a means of bringing deeper insight and understanding to their own specific work. School management needs good theories, and the best ones are those we derive from our own rich experience and apply to our practice.

We work in difficult times, as if, as a society, we have entered an evolutionary crisis in human affairs, a crisis characterized by a growing tension between scientific, technological and economic development and our capacity as citizens to lead secure, fulfilling and enriching lives. The twentieth century has been a period of rapid and accelerating change, gaining in momentum as we move inexorably into the new millennium. All organizations have felt the pressures of this crisis and some have recognized that the process of adaptation to new and often unexpected circumstances is the key to survival.

Our capacity to learn is perhaps the single most important element in this adaptive imperative, and we will need to apply much of the creativity and imagination we have focused on technology to our social and political world. The children now in our schools will need powerful new capabilities for their lives in the twenty-first century, and schools will have a truly crucial part to play in helping them to acquire those skills and qualities they will need to thrive and survive in a world which we can no longer predict for them.

The book examines the nature of management and leadership work in schools against a background of turbulence and confusion. After the somewhat rigid and mechanistic standardization of recent years, schools now need to rediscover the same creativity and imagination that enabled them to develop so significantly and successfully in previous times. We need a new wave of adaptive development that will take us forward with optimism and determination. The resources for success already lie within the schools, in their pupils and teachers. The necessary developments needed in these challenging times cannot be imposed from outside by legislation, enforced competition or fault-finding scrutiny. They will be achieved by those who have offered themselves as educators of the next generation. This book is about these educators and their work in the years ahead.

*Patrick Whitaker*

# List of figures

# Acknowledgements

The original ideas behind this book were developed in a series of conversations between Bob Croson and myself. The project was nearly abandoned when Bob had to drop out of the partnership. His original thinking, radical ideas and creative imagination have been a source of constant inspiration and energy over a period of nearly twenty years. In continuing the book alone I hope I have done justice to the plans we made, and that he finds much of himself in these pages. As a companion in the journey of learning, I dedicate the book to him.

# 1 Complexity and change

Chaos creates an affinity of patterns, and you never know what will happen next.
(Lewin, 1995)

## Introduction

At the time of writing, it is some weeks prior to a general election. The news reports the chaos of the transport system as coded messages warn of the dangers to the lives of ordinary travellers; the international community alerts itself to further tragedy in central Africa and the problems of political scandal in the Middle East; the *Times Educational Supplement* headlines the panic among headteachers to take early retirement before the opportunity is denied. We seem to live in a state of almost endemic turmoil in which our daily lives are worked out against a background of crisis and breakdown.

Those who work in schools are experiencing an increasing sense of frustration about the management of our schools. Teachers have absorbed an enormous range of changes to an already complex system, but have also experienced the society they serve seeming to turn on them, blaming them for all the current ills and difficulties of the nation. Schools seem to have become the scapegoat of a society ill at ease with itself, and confused about which direction it needs to take into the future. While we know that things are not as they used to be, we are not always clear why. Neither are we sure what we have to do to overcome our present difficulties. The future is unclear, prediction is hazardous and for many there seems little hope. As we become more aware of the dynamics of this evolutionary crisis, we will be in a better position to plan the adaptations required to survive the pressures that bear down and threaten us.

In our journey to the future, schools will have a vital part to play in this process of evolution and adaptation. The success of our future adults to adapt to the continuous change they will undoubtedly experience, will depend to a larger extent than in the past on the nature and quality of their earliest experiences in the schooling system. Our schools are a vital key to the future and it is essential that those who manage it are aware of the enormous impact that rapid and accelerating change can have on our lives.

This opening chapter is concerned with the turbulence within our schooling system. It deals with the impact of change on our schools and examines a range of factors which pose significant challenges to our work as leaders and managers. The chapter will:

- consider the nature of change in the late twentieth century
- explore a range of factors affecting our capacity to manage schools effectively
- examine the current climate within which education is currently conducted
- identify some dilemmas at the heart of educational management as we move towards both a new century and a new millennium.

---

Consider how your own circumstances have changed during your lifetime.

- What are now common features of your life that were not present in your childhood?
- In what ways has change affected you:
  - at home
  - at work
  - in your social life?
- What changes in the world are you particularly concerned about?
- In what ways are you actively working to promote change?

---

## The changing world

Many of us are currently experiencing a sense of disorientation in our lives, as if the future arrives before we are really ready for it. This creates an inexorable sense of crisis management in which somewhat haphazard events and incidents seem to run our lives, rather than our carefully formulated plans and intentions. Time management has become a major preoccupation as we struggle to cope.

Some of us hope and perhaps believe that a quieter golden age will eventually arrive, when things will calm down and there will be time to consolidate and reclaim deeply held beliefs. The indications are, however, that the pace of change will quicken rather than slow down.

Many who have been working in the education service over the past few years might claim that such a breakdown has already occurred. Tom Peters (1988), one of the foremost chroniclers of organizational change in recent years, acknowledges this desperate need for adaptive strategies in his book *Thriving on Chaos*. He suggests that we are faced with nothing less than a revolution in organizational and management practice, a revolution that necessarily needs to challenge everything we thought we knew about managing. 'Most fundamentally, the times

Box 1.1
*Future shock*
Alvin Toffler (1971) warned us a quarter of a century ago that the world was changing faster than ever before, and that the rapid acceleration of changes in all aspects of human activity would create a disorienting condition which he described as future shock.

He observed that:

- change is so powerful that it can overturn institutions, shift our values and shrivel our roots
- change is the process by which the future invades our lives
- the accelerating pace of change is an elemental force with personal, psychological as well as sociological consequences
- unless we can learn to control the rate of change we are doomed to a massive adaptational breakdown.

demand that flexibility and love of change replace our long standing penchant for mass production and mass markets, based as it is upon a relatively predictable environment now vanished' (Peters, 1988).

In recent years the theory of disordered structures has become a special interest to those who study the tendency to increasing complexity in our lives. Chaos theory has been created to try to find explanations for what we have assumed are disorderly structures in the world, but which on closer examination show remarkable signs of pattern and organization. It studies these apparently disorderly and unpredictable systems – those that are so haphazard that they do not appear to be governed by any laws (Talbot, 1996).

Human systems, such as schools, are certainly complex and increasingly we seem to experience them as chaotic. Most days we engage in a mixture of expected and unpredictable chain of events and situations that do not seem to be held together by any logical framework. The new fields of complexity theory and chaos theory

Box 1.2
*Chaos*
Tom Peters (1988), claims that chaos is the condition we have created for ourselves through our relentless pursuit of change and development.

Nothing less than a love affair with chaos, he argues, will enable the managers of the future to thrive.

Today, loving change, tumult, even chaos is a prerequisite for survival, let alone success.

have much to offer to those who have found the classical scientific theories altogether too tidy and mechanistic to explain the confusing patterns of events and behaviours present each day in school.

Charles Handy (1989) writing about this world of constant change, suggests that the epoch of intent, brought in with the Industrial Revolution, is now over and that we have entered the *age of unreason* in which the only prediction that will hold true is that no predictions will hold true. Observing the nature of change in recent years he notes:

- The changes are we are now experiencing are discontinuous and not part of an established pattern of change. This will be disturbing and disconcerting, particularly to those in power.
- Small changes will be particularly significant and may make the biggest differences to our lives.
- Discontinuous change will require discontinuous, upside down thinking to deal with it.

An environment in which fast and accelerating change is one of its most significant characteristics, poses a number of major challenges to those who manage schools. First, there is the general challenge – learning to live and cope with a world that is changing faster than we feel comfortable with. This is not simply a matter of increasing pace or workload, it is a more fundamental challenge to self-awareness, values, beliefs and vision. We have to acquire the capacity to know what it is vital to hold on to, and what to leave. To accompany this, we will need new skills, conceptual as well as practical, in order to thrive in a world of increasing complexity and confusion.

Second, we face a number of more specific challenges:

- to create school cultures that are optimistic, confident and future focused
- to develop a curriculum appropriate to a world of constant and accelerating change
- to prepare pupils for a future world that will be significantly different from the present
- to design management processes for schools that are more flexible, creative and open to continuous improvement.

In preparing for this future we need to bear in mind that:

- The pace of change will continue to accelerate.
- Managing ambiguity, complexity and paradox will become the significant challenges facing organizations.
- Insight, awareness and understanding of human activity will be more necessary than ever.
- The ability to thrive and survive will depend upon an increased capacity to adapt quickly to new conditions and situations.

The effective management of schools, indeed of all organizations, will demand a new sense of future consciousness – a capacity to focus on the complexities of change. It will be vital to spot significant trends and tendencies and to respond to them skilfully, developing an ability to adapt and modify systems, processes and structures as changed circumstances require.

These novel conditions create a range of confusions and dilemmas for those called upon to manage the education service. The Government, anxious to maintain a competitive edge in world markets, seems to be experiencing a deep confusion about how best to manage the education of the young in an increasingly fast-changing and turbulent world. Its response has been to set up a series of reforms to alter the structure and content of schooling. Sadly, it has tended to look to history for inspiration, to an age perceived as more certain, gentle, reassuring and successful. Nostrums from a mythical golden age are offered as alternatives to ideas that confront the increasingly confusing and uncertain future of which we are all part.

## Evolutionary challenges

Most of us are all too conscious of the tangible and visible changes around us, both in our own direct experience and across the world. What we are perhaps less aware of are the internal struggles and difficulties they create for us. Seven phenomena are especially significant:

- pressure
- complexity
- ambiguity
- uncertainty
- confusion
- turbulence
- stress.

### *Pressure*

Over recent years, schools have been subjected to a range of unprecedented pressures. These can be categorized as macro-pressures and micro-pressures.

---

*Box 1.3*
*Macro-pressures*
These are pressures affecting the whole world and include:

- rapid advances in science and technology
- ecological changes – global warming, atmospheric pollution, depletion of natural resources

- social changes – patterns of family life, drug cultures, unemployment, crime
- political changes – ethnic conflicts, breakdown of Soviet system, emancipation of South Africa
- huge developments in information technology.

*Micro-pressures*
These are closer to home and specific to education:

- devolved budgets to schools – LMS
- new types of schools – Grant Maintained and City Technology Colleges
- The National Curriculum
- new systems of accountability – teacher appraisal, assessment and testing
- systematic school inspection – OFSTED.

Macro-pressures impact on schools in two main ways:

1 They demand a curriculum which reflects these enormous trends and changes and which has the capacity to adapt quickly and flexibly to continuously changing situations.
2 They require schools to be a creative part of the change process itself, leading with new ideas and approaches finely tuned to emerging trends and developments.

Our schools now need to redeem the pioneering spirit that so characterized developments in education in the two decades after the Second World War.

Not only have the micro-pressures imposed enormous extra demands on an already under-resourced service, they have tended to diminish professional authority and create a culture of suspicion and mistrust.

These two types of pressure, in their powerful and different ways, have created a range of significant effects on the schools of the country, creating an altogether changed and changing context for the work of teachers and pupils.

Make a list of the micro-pressures which are currently affecting your own work in school.

What effects are these pressures having upon you?

## *Complexity*

Work and organizational life is now far more complex than it ever was. The huge growth in information and data – the rules, regulations, requirements, procedures, guidelines, policies and plans that affect our lives – have vastly extended the amount of detail that is required to operate the education service. Since the regulations themselves are complicated, they need circulars, explanations and guidance documents to support them. This creates a painful dilemma: whether to try to absorb, understand and assimilate them, or to rely on efficient systems of storage and retrieval. Whichever option is adopted, more time and energy than ever before has to be allocated to the management of information and data.

---

*Box 1.4*
*Complexity*
Two aspects of complexity are relevant:

1 Information complexity
   Information is increasing all the time and demanding an ever extending filing system to accommodate it. Computer systems are now marketed on the size of their storage capacity and their ability to process enormous quantities of data.
2 Dynamic complexity
   The human activity now required to manage all this information and make sense of it.

---

No sooner, it seems, than we have accommodated the most recent update than a new one arrives to replace it. In its short life, the National Curriculum has already been through many changes, modifications, radical revisions and updates. It is easy to blame lack of foresight. In a fast-changing world we must learn not to be quite so surprised that changes are already being planned before previous programmes are fully implemented. We need to adjust to shorter shelf-lives for projects and decisions, and perhaps not try to make things so perfect that they will last for ever.

Few of us were socialized or educated for complexity. The strictures in our childhoods were for simplicity and straightforwardness, always to seek the single correct solution to a problem. We were led to believe that if we think hard enough we will be able to keep things tidy and properly accounted for. We were encouraged to seek out the main points and not worry too much about the subsidiary ones. In these demanding times it is frustrating not to have simple solutions, but it is only slowly dawning on us that most complex problems have complex causes, and that the search for the single most important one will probably leave the problem unsolved. Arguments about causes of crime, class size in schools and the problems of drugs become polarized by the debate between the espousers of alternative simple solutions to complexity.

One of the great educational challenges facing us is how to help the children now in our schools to grow up with a capacity to manage complexity more successfully than older generations seem able to do.

## *Ambiguity*

During the last two decades we have moved into an information world where meanings are often ambiguous. Language strains to sustain a capacity for clarity, as detail becomes ever more complicated and intricate. Technical language and jargon becomes increasingly necessary to provide specificity of definition, and words in common parlance are taken to embrace particular and technical meanings. Global communication requires a common language, but until that is achieved translation will be problematical, as many of us who have struggled with translated instructions to self-assembly furniture will testify.

As the world becomes more tightly regulated and more precisely defined, more and more people will be engaged in the business of spelling things out. Regulations themselves can often be quite brief, but the guidance and interpretation that needs to accompany them can stretch to many volumes. The recent corrections to a railway timetable were longer than the original timetable itself. This means that most of us are having to allocate time from our prime responsibilities into the process of seeking clarification and understanding. And herein lies a real human predicament. Many of us have come to believe that our seeming incapacity to keep abreast of data is an indication of a significant decline in our intellectual capacities, so we tend to blame ourselves and feel ashamed of our increasingly limited abilities.

---

*Box 1.5*
*Ambiguity*
A few years ago, as this ambiguity phenomenon began to create a growing sense of discomfort, the following epithet was doing the rounds on posters and cards:

> 'I know you believe you
> understand what you think I
> said, but I am not sure you
> realize that what you heard is
> not what I meant.'

Can you say this in a simpler way?

---

Since much of the documentary data is generated by people with sectional concerns and specific interests, much of it is detailed and technical. For those working in schools, much of the information is ambiguous, relying on previous knowledge or other documentation. This creates more work, because readers have to check with others whether their understanding is the correct one, requiring more phone calls, personal interruptions and time-consuming deliberation.

That we need to learn to adjust to the increasingly paradoxical and contradictory nature of life is clear and we must learn not to be surprised by the the inconsistencies we encounter in our daily lives. Complexity breeds ambiguity and creates perplexity. Perhaps it is bewilderment which is now the sign of a really first-rate intelligence. As educators, we find ourselves simultaneously struggling with the presence of ambiguity in our own lives as we try to help pupils to cope with it more imaginatively and effectively in theirs.

> Consider the range of ambiguities and paradoxes that affect your life, particularly at work.
>
> What difficulties do these ambiguities create for you and how do you handle them?

### Uncertainty

As Charles Handy (1989) has observed, the only safe prediction is that any prediction is unsafe. Teachers were led to believe that the National Curriculum was here to stay, and so set about implementing it with energy and determination, only to discover that it was to undergo almost perpetual alteration and modification. Uncertainty about which version to use, and whether to wait until the next one arrives has pervaded the lives of teachers. Sir Ron Dearing was called in to resolve this dilemma, but in such a rapidly changing world the whole idea of a rigidly prescriptive curriculum is questionable anyway. Constant change and adaptation will continue to be necessary, and these dilemmas will continue until the schools themselves are left to manage modification and development for themselves.

Post-modern perspectives try to explain this end of an era phenomenon. They note that the characteristics of the world are now the disintegration of traditional structures and the breakdown of the big ideas that have sustained our evolution – the truth of scientific discovery, continuous economic growth, the capacity of technology to rescue us from our misguided excesses. What we are witnessing in the world of state-funded education is the fragmentation of traditional monolithic structures. The system has become more diverse and less

---

*Box 1.6*

*Uncertainty*

One of the characteristics of the modern world is that the predictions we were once urged to place reliance on, no longer work. It is increasingly difficult to tell our children what they can expect in their lifetimes.

Life spans of over 100 years are becoming more common and there may be children now in our schools whose lives will last from the end of the twentieth century to the beginning of the twenty-second.

What exactly can we tell them about what their lives will be like in 2006 let alone 2106?

---

subject to consistency and similarity of pattern. The difference now is that we know these changes will not last as long as the structure created by the 1944 Education Act. In the past decade we have had more educational legislation than in the whole previous history of state managed schooling. The recent changes we are involved in implementing, will themselves be subject to continuous waves of alteration and modification. New ideas will need to be put in place quicker, and will last for a shorter time than before. Continuous development and improvement is the process replacing occasional change events.

In the future, we will need to place less reliance on detailed long-term plans, perhaps holding on to our value-based dreams and visions of how we want things to be while we create the plans and programmes that will get us through the next few weeks and months. This will place a new emphasis on a rather loosely defined aspect of human capability – *living on your wits*. This will need to be introduced into the formal curriculum for schools if the adults of the future are to succeed in avoiding the debilitating effects of complexity, uncertainty and confusion. Those with a capacity to work imaginatively and creatively in the moment will be the key assets of any organization. This does not imply that reckless management will replace planned development, but that we will need to attach a greater importance to the skills of managing in the heat of the moment, dealing with whole varieties of issues that no amount of planning can predict.

How does uncertainty manifest itself in your role, particularly in your work with colleagues and pupils?

What do your consider to be the implications for schools in an increasingly uncertain future?

### Confusion

Confusion is perhaps the single most prevalent phenomenon in most schools, and one of the greatest challenges to those in senior management positions. Few people enjoy being confused, and strive to overcome their feelings of panic, disorientation, uncertainty and despair. We will need to learn to be more comfortable with the inevitable confusions that the modern world and its accelerating pace of change imposes. Although we do not like to feel confused we are even more reluctant to confess that we are, so we wander round our schools feeling dazed while pretending to be clear.

An organization staffed with people who are pretending to know is a nightmare that can only be overcome by learning to live with confusion, and to accept its inevitable presence in our lives. Indeed, the most dangerous person in the organization of the future will be the person who claims not to be confused. In the future it may be certainty that we need to be wary of.

The problem with confusion is partly to do with our upbringing. We learn to regard the presence of confusion in our lives as a deficiency of intellect, a weakness in our minds. People who demonstrate confusion are often referred to as *not very bright*. Clarity and single-mindedness are regarded as the mark of a superior intelligence. No wonder so

---

*Box 1.7*
*Confusion*
If we do experience life as difficult it is because it is, not that we are deficient.

M. Scott Peck (1985) addressing the pathologies of the modern world begins his book *The Road Less Travelled*, with an almost heretical assertion: 'Life is difficult.'

He goes on to explain his thinking:

This is a great truth, one of the greatest truths. It is a great truth because once we really see this truth, we transcend it. Once we truly know that life is difficult – once we truly understand and accept it – then life is no longer difficult. Because once it is accepted, the fact that life is difficult no longer matters.

Most do not fully see this truth that life is difficult. Instead they moan more or less incessantly, noisily or subtly, about the enormity of their problems, their burdens, and their difficulties as if life were generally easy, as if life should be easy. They voice their belief noisily or subtly, that their difficulties represent a unique kind of affliction that should not be and that has somehow been visited especially upon them. I know about this moaning because I have done my share.

many of us struggle to conceal our confusions. The conclusion we usually come to when we experience confusion is that we are just not clever enough, and we rue the belief that if only we had worked harder at school, and paid attention to the exhortations of our teachers, we would be freed from the paralysing ineptness we can so often experience. This is a most dangerous perception and one that can hold us back from the proper sense of achievement and well-being, so vital to the effective discharge of our roles and responsibilities.

Shifting our thinking to this more radical but reassuring viewpoint will not be comfortable. For many of us the self-perception of inadequacy is deeply ingrained and it will not easily be relinquished.

One of the most important focuses for staff development and appraisal in the future, will be to share and disclose with our colleagues the nature of our own professional dilemmas and difficulties. As the pace of change intensifies, so we will need to allocate even more specific periods of time to the vital process of deliberate reflection on our professional experience.

To accompany this we will need to accept the presence of confusion in our lives as an indication of the complexity that we are required to deal with. Confessing to confusion will come to be seen as a sign of strength rather than weakness. Perhaps only those genuinely in touch with their own confusion can claim to be living in the so-called *real world*.

> What sort of confusions do you experience in your work? How do you handle these?
>
> In what ways do you help colleagues and pupils who are experiencing confusion but trying not to show it?

### Turbulence

Some indication of the real experience of people at work can be gleaned from the metaphors they use to explain the essence of their job. Frequently employed is the notion of moving goalposts – the loss of clear targets, the relentless changing of direction and priority. When a sense of purpose is absent, then inevitably purposelessness ensues. Some speak about keeping the plates spinning – a hard enough task when there are only a very few, a nightmare when new ones are added by the hour. Others refer to the increasing speed of the treadmill and note how difficult it becomes to step off when the pace really speeds up. Most of us have found our personal lives invaded by work – tasks that cannot be undertaken in the relentless turbulence of school life being taken home to be done when we would be better relaxing.

Box 1.8
*Turbulence*
It is an increasingly common experience for us to arrive at the end of a working day totally exhausted but confused about what it is we have achieved. We arrive at work in the mornings with our lists of important things to do and find that by the end of the day, despite our frantic busyness, few of the items have been attended to.

Henry Mintzberg (1973) in his study of the work patterns of organizational managers noted the turbulent complexity of their work, observing that most managers spend their time in an endless sequence of short interactions – rarely longer than eight or nine minutes – few of which they had any prior knowledge.

Most teachers too, in the managing of pupil learning, experience this pattern with its haphazardness and unpredictability. The trouble is we have been led to believe that good managers are proactive, successfully steering themselves elegantly through a sequence of predetermined tasks.

Busy organizations, especially complex ones like schools, create a plethora of human needs which require to be satisfied if the work of the organization is to succeed. The real work of managers is to expect these wants and needs, and to respond to them vigorously and sensitively. For too long we have worked on the assumption that admitting to a need is a sign of incompetence, and so we have conspired to limit and inhabit the true potential of the organization and the creative people within it. School life is turbulent, conducted at a furious pace. Given the dynamics created by complexity, uncertainty and confusion we have to learn that the documentary and strategic aspects of management have to be conducted when the turbulence has quietened down, and where the opportunity of quality time becomes possible – not an easy option for managers in the modern educational system.

Most of us are aware of this turbulence and its effects on our lives. It can be described as change that accelerates faster than our capacity to keep pace with it comfortably. It feels as if we run a constant risk of being left behind and our inadequacies exposed to ridicule and condemnation because we have not tried hard enough. We are faced with agonizing choices – work harder, faster and longer or, as they say – go to the wall. Few deliberately choose this latter option since they have no investment in failure, until it is too late, and the costs of being in overdrive for too long take their toll on our health and sanity. Sadly it is often the most committed and effective in our profession who end their careers in exhaustion and disillusionment.

It is here that the evolutionary crisis is most painfully felt. We may know we have to adapt to survive, but few of us know what precise form the adaptation needs to take. There is no shortage of advice – *work smarter, not harder,* the management gurus tell us – but they give no practical indication of what we should do, nor do they tell us about the worries, anxieties and guilt that is often created when we try to give up the habits of a lifetime. It is very hard to adopt new approaches when those with power and influence over us are determined to judge us by the old ones. It will take great courage to embark on this necessary process of transformation and adaptation. It is unlikely to be achieved unless those at the top of organizational hierarchies lead by example and let go of the assumptions, attitudes and practices that we have sustained for too long in a changed and changing world. They will need to give the highest priority to their own adaptation, and also provide support and encouragement of the highest quality to their over-demanded colleagues. The journey through the evolutionary crisis has to be led by senior staff who recognize that it is their own working practices that may need changing the most.

> How does uncertainty manifest itself in your role, particularly in your work with colleagues and pupils?
>
> What do your consider to be the implications for schools in an increasingly uncertain future?

## Stress

The combined effect of these features is another more insidious outcome – increased stress and psychological discomfort. Studies into occupational stress show teachers to be among the higher risk groups, and each year an increasing number of working days are lost through stress-related illnesses.

While some stress is a necessary prerequisite for effective human activity, it can become particularly dangerous when individual staff members experience a growing gap between the work they are required to do and the time and energy required to do it in. More personal time has to be spent on job-related activity, placing in jeopardy social well-being, family cohesion and personal health.

For too long, occupational stress has been regarded as a matter for the individual who experiences it and, often, as an indicator of incompetence or lack of commitment. Senior staff in schools need to recognize that stress is a management issue, and something which management processes have the capacity to increase or reduce. The key resource for any organization is the arrival at work each day of staff who are physically fit and healthy, energetic and optimistic, and with a sense of psychological well-being. At present this is not true of the majority of teachers.

In what circumstances do you experience stress? What combination of factors cause this stress? How do you handle it?

What sorts of stress do you notice in your colleagues? How do they handle it? What is your response when you see your colleagues suffering in this way?

The combined effect of these seven phenomena is to fuel frustration, guilt and self-doubt, dangerously sapping professional optimism, competence and ambition. Being a senior manager in this sort of social and psychological context, when you too are experiencing similar pressures and stresses, is not a job for the faint-hearted. Management work is becoming more and more difficult and demanding and there are no easy fixes or quick solutions to the succession of challenges and dilemmas that present themselves daily in our schools.

Part of the challenge lies in the fact that, despite Toffler's warnings and the exhortations of Peters and Handy, we have not yet adapted our cultural and interpersonal ideas sufficiently well to cope with a world characterized by conflicts, imperatives, exhortations and a sense of unworthiness.

All our preparation and training for the management work we are now required to do was for a different world, one with more certainties and less confusions. Our childhood upbringing, education and training has left us unprepared and insufficiently equipped for the world we have inherited. The only answer is to become learners again, tuned into the ambiguities and paradoxes that now so characterize the world of work and organizations. As Peters (1992) has said in his most recent study of organizational life: 'People who are uncomfortable in an unstructured world, won't make it.'

We need to recognize that our successes and achievements as managers and leaders will depend more on what we learn while doing the job, than what we have brought with us from the past. The inherited beliefs, assumptions and principles which have formed the basis for management activity since the beginning of the century have to be challenged and confronted. Nothing short of a major shift in our management thinking, and a fundamental change in the relationships between senior staff and the rest, is likely to produce organizational effectiveness in the increasingly complex times to come.

## Educational change

It is unfortunate that so much of what happens in education is affected by the competitive ethic – being brighter than someone else, getting higher marks, achieving a landmark first. It applies in the rivalry between the state and private sectors, and now within the state sector itself as Local Management of Schools (LMS) links school survival with pupil recruitment. One of the common polarized arguments hinges on the belief by one side that competition is the essence of progress, and the belief by the other that competition merely sustains inequality of opportunity and inhibits successful learning. A concern with rivalry – of winning, or at least not losing – can cloud attention to the more fundamental purposes of education.

A great deal of change in education has had a reform element about it. The assumption that changing the structure of schooling is the way to ensure improved learning is still the belief of many politicians. While improvement is constantly needed, it is sad that many of the reasons forwarded for wishing to improve are so connected with tangential issues – to be better than other countries, to prove experts wrong, to increase the competitiveness of British industry, or because standards are different to what they were fifty years ago. In all this there seems a reluctance to grasp the essential fact – that the world is different to what it was, and is changing fast. For an educational system to be in tune with change it needs to be flexible, adaptable and responsive to constantly changing circumstances and needs.

The obsession with current deficits and difficulties does nothing to advance the idea of an educational system for a changing world. It merely deepens prejudices, further polarizes positions and keeps the debate focused on what exists now, rather than on the visions of what it will need to be like in ten or twenty years time.

Nowhere in the current round of reform is there present the notion that the most appropriate change is continuous and systematic improvement, in which change is seen as a constant process of building and developing, rather than an event to be engaged in with great energy when things have got really bad. If schools cannot be trusted to change for themselves, then intermittent flurries of activity will be necessary. As the pace of change in the world accelerates these flurries will become more urgent and more insistent, and sadly, increasingly dysfunctional.

One of the difficulties facing those charged with the management of schools is the rigid context for education envisaged by the reformers. Educational change is approached in strictly rational terms as a choice between opposing alternatives, only one of which is right. This manifestly fails to realize that education and learning is characterized by complexity and an infinite range of variables. Simple solutions must be at worst wrong and at best partial.

Those responsible for the direction of educational policy need to realize what an increasing number of commercial organizations have already realized – that survival and development in a fast-changing world depends upon simultaneity rather than exclusion. Polarized patterns of thinking automatically exclude certain variables and include others – the either/or approach to change. Creative solutions

Box 1.9

*Divergence and variety*

Ashby's Law of Requisite Variety (Garratt, 1987) suggests that for an organization to survive and develop, there must be sufficient difference within it to allow it to cope with change.

The pursuit of monolithic structures will produce too much similarity, thus reducing the ability of the organization to learn and adapt to a rapidly changing environment.

While a variety of perspectives and viewpoints can be more difficult to manage than everyone thinking in the same way, it can result in decisions being taken with insufficient information and imagination. In fast-changing times, turbulent creativity has to be preferred to management comfort and simple like-mindedness.

will undoubtedly include some elements of both positions – divergence and variation will demand it. There needs to be sufficient variety of policy and practice to make development possible.

Education is a synthesis – a bringing together of knowledge, ideas, possibilities and practicalities. Its very essence is experience and the meaning that is construed through reflection on that experience. There is very little reflection in the current debate among the protagonists. Successful change requires reflection as well as reaction, thinking as well as doing, and vision and imagination as much as intellect and belief.

# The educational dilemma

Recent developments in education have emphasized performance above all things. What seems to count for most in the political debate about schooling is that pupils at each stage of their education can demonstrate formal competence on a rather narrow range of skills and abilities. It is sad that almost no attention at all is paid to the importance of education as an unfolding of potential, a striving for identity and understanding and a search for happiness and fulfilment. What really seems to count most is how children behave when they are tested, not how they think or feel, or what their ambitions in life are.

This struggle between appearance and essence endangers the very process of education. At their best, schools have held both as self-evident, recognizing that the true education of the human being has full regard for all its potentialities. It is deeply depressing that the polarity of the traditional/progressive schism also reflects this distinction. What effective educators have always recognized is that in the process of learning, you cannot have one without the other. It is a matter of synthesis, not of separation.

The protracted and disputatious debate about the detail of the National Curriculum has revealed the tendency to see success as making the right choices – whether knowledge is more important than skill, design of the curriculum more important than its delivery or structure more relevant than process. The problem lies in the creating of false dichotomies and the posing of dilemmas. These vital issues affecting the management and development of formal learning in schools cannot be reduced to questions of *either/or*. What is needed is an acceptance that all are important and that each has an appropriate and significant contribution to make to the whole. What is equally vital is that we learn to appreciate that it is the relationships between these necessary contributory parts that holds the key to change and improvement. Until we realize that the key to understanding human affairs and activities lies more in making connections between the various factors, than in struggling to define a pecking order of relative importance, we are unlikely to satisfy our desperate need to raise the quality of learning in schools.

---

Where do you stand on the issues discussed in this final section of the chapter?

What do you see as the way forward for schools in the next few years?

---

Look at the notes you have made during your reflections throughout this chapter.

Do you feel optimistic about the future? Do you see the challenges ahead as interesting and exciting, or as fearful and depressing?

What are your own resources for the challenges ahead? What skills and qualities can you offer to school leadership in the years to come?

# 2 Defining the task

Some problems are just too complicated for rational logical solutions.
They admit of insights, not answers.
(Weisner, quoted in Boot, Lawrence and Morris, 1994)

## Introduction

One of the first activities for anyone in a management role is to
determine what needs to be done. Before tasks can be defined and
programmes of action prepared, it is necessary to review current
circumstances, purposes, plans, activities and outcomes.

This chapter focuses on the management work required to take
stock of what is happening in a school, or in an area of specific
management responsibility, so that decisions about what needs to be
done can be made. It offers some ways of thinking about school
management and outlines some ways of approaching the stocktaking
exercise.

The chapter will:

- consider the differences and similarities between schools and other
  types of organization
- examine some differences between leadership and management
- discuss the question of what schools are for
- explore the processes involved in taking stock of current activity
- introduce a conceptual framework of the key aspects of school
  management
- offer a practical approach to the carrying out of a management
  review.

- Reflect on your current role. What aspects of management and
  leadership does it cover?
- Make a list of the active verbs which describe what you are
  expected to do in this role.
- How is your role defined? What do you consider to be its key
  emphasis and focus?
- Complete the sentence – The main purpose of my job is to . . .

## Schools as organizations

Organizations are the driving force for virtually all our country's economic and technological endeavours and a great deal of our social activity too. Three particular features are common to all organizations:

1 They exist in social settings and consist of a complex network of roles, relationships and interactions.
2 They are purposeful. They exist to serve particular intentions, functions and purposes.
3 They are managed. The activities of the people working in them need to be planned, co-ordinated and evaluated.

Schools share these characteristics with all other types of organization, but have some distinctive features of their own:

- They are life centred, concerned with the experiences and daily life of children and young people.
- They aim to facilitate the processes of human growth and development.
- Success in their work is significantly more difficult to measure and analyse than the outcomes of more product-based organizations.

The complexities of schooling are affected by three factors which influence the management process more than they do in most other types of organization:

1 *Philosophy* Questions of how and why children learn are the subject of continuous debate and enquiry. Differing and sometimes entrenched positions create significant challenges to the management processes in schools.
2 *Politics* During the second half of the twentieth century, schooling has become the subject of considerable competition between political parties, and schools have become victims of intense and often acrimonious disputes between the parties as to how schools should be managed.
3 *Tradition* There continues within the teaching profession, and indeed beyond it, a vigorous debate about purposes for education and methodology.

Perhaps the most significant factor about a school as an organization lies in the fact that schooling is a human process, concerned with growth, change and development. This means that virtually all its systems and processes revolve around the thoughts, feelings, experiences and behaviours of people. The leadership and management of

*Box 2.1*
*Four broad traditions in education*
(Walford, 1981)
1 The liberal humanitarian tradition which is primarily concerned with passing on the basic cultural heritage from one generation to another.
2 The pupil-centred tradition which values self-development, self-reliance and social harmony for the individual learner.
3 The utilitarian tradition which sees the main job of education as equipping students to go well prepared into an already defined future.
4 The reconstructionalist tradition which sees education as a potential instrument for changing society.

---

*Box 2.2*
*What are pupils?*
Handy and Aitken (1986) suggest that children pose a dilemma because it is not clear how they relate to the organization. Are they workers, products or clients?

- A worker is a member of an organization who co-operates in a joint endeavour.
- A product is the output, which is shaped and developed by the organization.
- A client is a beneficiary of an organization, who is served by the endeavour.

In some ways, they suggest, the child is all three, but each has a different emphasis in different phases of schooling:

*Primary schools*
Children are predominantly workers, grouped together in one place with one supervisor carrying out tasks.

*Secondary schools*
Pupils are predominantly products, working for perhaps ten supervisors in one week, in maybe ten different locations in a variety of groupings. There is no one place the pupil can call their own and all belongings have to be carried around in a bag.

*Sixth forms*
Students are predominatly clients, with the school as provider of resources. The student is largely independent and self-directing with access to a wide range of services.

human processes is extremely complex and is influenced and affected by a phenomenally wide range of constantly changing variables.

Handy and Aitken (1986) emphasize the ambiguity of these organizational factors:

> Schools are different because of the children. It makes a vast difference whether teachers see themselves as independent professionals with clients, as managers of groups of cooperating workers or as shapers of products in the making. To claim to be one and then inadvertently to act the other turns schools into pretences where reality undermines idealism. Teachers often have a deep moral and personal commitment to their pupils; it would shock many of them to hear these spoken of as 'products' and to be told that, organizationally, the process of their school was akin to an old fashioned factory. Actions, however, override rhetoric; the way we organize our schools, particularly our secondary schools, dictates the way the child sees the teacher. It is as important to understand organizations as it is to understand children or to know your subject.

A final factor to consider is that schools are staffed by professionals, all of whom have qualified through academic and professional training to practise. Professional autonomy is a strong tradition in schooling and creates a different management climate than that experienced in other types of organization. As Donald Schon (1983) observes: 'Practitioners are frequently embroiled in conflicts of values, goals, purposes and interests. Teachers are faced with pressures for increased efficiency in the context of contracting budgets, demands that they rigorously 'teach the basics', exhortations to to encourage creativity, build citizenship, help students to examine their values.'

Given both the range of similarities between schools and other kinds of organization, and the distinctive and significant differences referred to above, we can see that the processes of leadership and management will pose a range of demanding challenges to all those with professional responsibilities in school.

---

- How do you see the relationship between schools and other organizations?
- Where do you stand in terms of the four traditions outlined in Box 2.1?
- How do you view the pupils in relation to the Handy and Aitken classification in Box 2.2?

# Leadership and management

The terms 'management' and 'leadership' are often used inter-changeably. While there are considerable similarities between the two concepts it can be useful to make a distinction between the emphasis of each.

---

Box 2.3
Defining terms
Management is mainly concerned with:

- keeping the organization running
- orderly structures
- maintaining day-to-day functions
- ensuring that work gets done
- monitoring outcomes and results
- organizational efficiency.

Leadership is more especially concerned with:

- personal and interpersonal behaviour
- focus on the future
- visions and purposes
- change and development
- quality of outcome
- achievement and success
- personal effectiveness.

---

These are descriptive distinctions and are not intended to imply that leadership is more important than management. Rather the distinction is intended to emphasize a growing understanding of the human and interactive aspects of organizations. Management activity is necessary to keep the organization functioning efficiently, so that plans come to fruition, procedures work and objectives are met. Leadership is concerned with creating conditions in which all members of the organization can give of their best in a climate of commitment and challenge. Management enables an organization to function, leader-ship helps it to work well.

Throughout this book 'management' is used as a generic term, referring to all those activities concerned with the successful running of a school. 'Leadership' will be used specifically to refer to the interpersonal dimension of managers' work and will be discussed in more detail in Chapters 4 and 7.

> - What specific distinctions would you make between management and leadership?
> - Identify some of the work you have undertaken in the last few days. Which activities have been of a distinctly management nature? Which have had a specifically leadership element about them?
> - Consider your colleagues. How do you distinguish between the two aspects in the ways they conduct their roles?

## What are schools for?

In recent years, debates about education have tended to focus on two perceived problems:

1 That as a nation the achievements of our schools as measured by examination results have seemed to slip below those of other nations.
2 That a National Curriculum is necessary to ensure uniformity of content and entitlement.

These twin imperatives have tended to dominate the educational debate in recent years. Other important aspects have been ignored, and these also need to be addressed if the work of educational managers is to be driven by purpose rather than panic.

Our management work will involve us in philosophical, ideological and political issues. It will also require us to deal with hard-edged practicalities and stark choices. Given the enormous range and complexity of the landscape of school management, it is vital to create some maps and frameworks which can help us to find the way (Figure 2.1).

| PURPOSE | POLICY | PRACTICE | PRODUCT |

*Figure 2.1*  The 4P development chain

### Purpose

The purpose link of the chain is concerned with why we need schools and what it is that we want children to learn about in them. Most of us can quickly come up with a range of purposes:

- to meet the social and economic needs of society
- to enable children to learn about the world

- to facilitate access to the world of work
- to transmit social and cultural traditions
- to provide a foundation for adult life.

It is because many of these purposes seem self-evident that they have not been seen as an issue in recent years, and yet major changes in society would suggest that our sense of purpose for schooling should at least be reviewed. One sensible way to behave when faced with a crisis is to return to fundamental questions about purpose. Not only is it vital for the nation as a whole to be addressing purpose, it is crucial for individual schools to be doing it as well. It is virtually impossible for any management work to be purposeful unless we can endow it with purpose. Purpose is the driving force for most worthwhile activities in life, and is a key element in the management of schools.

Neil Postman (1997) has suggested that those who run education at the highest level have become obsessed with objectives and targets and have tended to ignore purpose altogether. In a fast-changing world, he argues, those concerned with the future of schools need to be constantly revising their purposes.

He offers two purposes for our consideration. The first he calls the story of the 'Spaceship Earth':

---

*Box 2.4*
*Spaceship Earth*
This is the story of human beings as stewards of the earth, caretakers of a vulnerable space capsule. It is relatively new narrative, not fully developed, that evokes in young people a sense of responsibility and commitment. And it is a story that has the power to bind people. It makes the idea of racism both irrelevant and ridiculous, and it makes clear the interdependence of human beings and their need for solidarity. If any part of the spaceship is poisoned, then all suffer; which is to say that the extinction of the rain forest is not a Brazilian problem, the problem of the oceans is not a Miami problem, the depletion of the ozone layer is not an Australian problem.

This is an idea whose time has come. It is a story of interdependence and global co-operation, of what is at the core of humanness; a story that depicts waste and indifference as evil, that requires a vision of the future and a commitment to the present.

---

If we were to take this purpose story seriously, then undoubtedly some reworking of the National Curriculum would be necessary as would some rethinking of the continuing traditions of teaching methodology.

> *Box 2.5*
> *The story of human error*
> The major theme of the story is that human beings make mistakes. All the time. It is our nature to make mistakes. We can scarcely let an hour go by without making one.

The second narrative Postman calls 'The story of human error'.

What pupils have tended to be faced with in school is the necessity for mistake avoidance. Traditionally, schooling has been about getting things right or wrong, and right is good and wrong is bad. Postman (1997) goes on to say that if we also took this story of human error seriously then: 'we would have a curriculum that does not see knowledge as a fixed commodity, but as an ongoing struggle to overcome human error. In fact the curriculum would be the study of error and our heroic efforts to overcome it.' Such a curriculum would have as its purpose to cure ourselves of the belief in absolute knowledge, and to promote the idea that we are dangerous to ourselves and others when we aspire to the knowledge of the gods.

Attention to purpose is a fundamental part of our work as managers and we need to engage in thinking and talking about what Postman calls the metaphysical basis of schooling, so that we can find purposes that are worthy of such an expensive and time-consuming enterprise. He ends his article with a challenging assertion: 'without a transcendent and honourable purpose, schooling must come to an end, and the sooner we are done with it the better. With such a purpose, schooling becomes the central institution through which the young may find reasons to educate themselves' (Postman, 1997).

The purpose link in the development chain is not only useful for drawing large philosophical issues to our attention, it offers us a conceptual structure we can use on almost any management issue or task.

- What for you are the purposes for education?
- What specific purposes are schools best able to serve?
- How would you define your own purposes as an educator?

## Policy

Once we have determined our purposes, the policy link in the chain takes us a stage further. Here we need to define our commitments and articulate what we intend to do. In recent years policy-making in schools has tended to become focused on the requirements of the OFSTED framework, and it is important that it is not seen only in this limited way. Our policies announce what we believe in, what visions we have for the future, our intentions for pupils and what it is we want them to achieve.

- What policies currently drive the management work of your organization?
- What responsibilities do you have for policy-making in your own role?
- How in your school are policy commitments communicated to those who will benefit from them?

## Practice

If the purpose link is concerned with reasons and the policy link with commitments, then the practice link is concerned with action and how the purposes and policies can be transformed into desired products. This is the strategic territory of management and leadership and involves the planning, implementing and evaluating of school policies and plans.

The study of organizational management, like schooling itself, has a turbulent history and has experienced similar ideological disputes. The literature of management is full of competing claims, theories, methodologies and techniques, and this book is no exception. All of us who write about, or practise the art of management, have our beliefs about the best ways to proceed. In the face of the evolutionary crisis referred to in the previous chapter we shall need to dig deep within our own experiences to examine traditional orthodoxies with a critical eye, and to develop our own pathways into the future.

- What are the active elements of your management role?
- In what ways are you involved in all four links of the development chain?
- Use the development chain as an analytical tool to place the different aspects of the management of your organization in its systematic sequence.

## Product

The product link is concerned with what we want the outcomes of the schooling process to be. Current beliefs in this country place almost obsessive emphasis on knowledge-based attainment – particularly as measured by Standard Assessment Tests (SATs) at the end of the first three key stages, and by public examinations in Key Stage 4. It is interesting to consider what product ideas a nation might hold that would be different from these and more in line with the purpose stories outlined by Neil Postman. Fortunately we have an example.

---

Box 2.6
*Norwegian schools*
In 1994 the Norwegian Department of Education produced a statement of outcome ambitions for school-leavers:

- a person searching for meaning
- a creative person
- a working person
- an enlightened person
- a co-operating person
- an environmentally friendly person.

---

What a stunning contrast there is between this bold and forward-looking statement and our own somewhat utilitarian and life-diminishing aspirations for children. It is a sobering thought to consider that with a continual extension of life expectancy some of the children now entering our primary schools will not only be alive throughout the twenty-first century, a significant number of them will still be alive into the twenty-second century. Will our current ambitions, based on an understanding of today's world still be relevant to those living in the changed circumstances of the late twenty-first century?

The product link in the development chain draws attention to what it is we are producing. It is both the final link in the chain, but can also be used as the first if we work in reverse order and embark on a review exercise. This development chain provides a simple and systematic guide to our management work.

- How are the intended outcomes of your own organization defined?
- What are your thoughts about the Norwegian statement?
- How do you articulate your own role aspirations and how do you assess your own successes and achievements?

# What needs doing?

In these days of fast change and constant innovation, a great deal of management work involves moving things forward. When we take up a new post there usually is an expectation that we will do things differently from our predecessors, and we are keen to demonstrate our management skills on new projects and developments. Whether we are taking up a headship, a curriculum co-ordinator post or a class teaching position, we will need to prepare ourselves for change – the movement from our present place to a different place at some stage in the future (Figure 2.2).

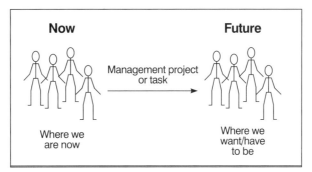

*Figure 2.2* Managing a project

Development needs to be the constant and continuous driving force of school life. In the fast-changing times in which we now live, striving for stability is a forlorn ambition, and effective managers are those who can work with a clear vision in mind, but also with an acute sensitivity to the turbulence of the educational environment in which they work with its unpredictability and uncertainty.

This inevitably involves a tendency to *short-termism*, working to tighter deadlines and shorter innovation timetables. Trying to get things right in the design stage is fraught with difficulties, since the circumstances which gave rise to the design need may well alter again before the design itself is completed. This creates a challenge to our working metabolism, where we have conceived of major development projects in terms of years, rather than months or weeks. Today, we need to get things up and running much more quickly before other competing requirements rush in to demand our attention.

## Sizing up the tasks ahead

There are a variety of questions which we need to ask in order to provide ideas about what needs to be done, either when we take up a new post, or when we are faced with a new project:

- Where are we now?
- Where have we come from?
- Is where we are where we intended to be?
- How well are we doing?
- Where do we need to go next?
- How are we feeling about where we are?
- Do we have a plan?

The answers to these and similar questions provide us with the information we need to establish intention, determine future action, set direction, establish priorities and get started. More precise questions than those posed above require us to make comparisons and engage in judgement:

- Is the previously stated destination still relevant?
- Is the destination actually specified?
- Have we reached the destination, gone beyond it or are we still on the journey?
- Is this organization working to specified objectives with clearly established success criteria?

The attempt to discover the present state of things is not simply a matter of articulating answers to these questions, it is more a process of setting up lines of enquiry which provide the means of deciding what courses of action may be necessary. It is important to make a distinction between two meanings behind the questions:

1 How does this school work?
2 How well is it doing?

The first question attempts to unravel something about subjective reality – how the organization is perceived and experienced by those who are associated with it. The second is more concerned with objective reality and the ways in which the organization is succeeding in serving its declared purposes and achieving its stated aims. Both meanings are vital, although it is the second which seems to be the driving force behind the current obsession with hard-edged accountability. How members of an organization feel about their work and its outcomes is as important to managers as the precise nature of behavioural performance at any one time. It is the neglect of the subjective dimension which has led to so much dispute and conflict in organizations over the past 200 years or so.

The key purpose behind these questions is to provide the information that will enable current managers to orientate themselves to their responsibilities and to the direction which the organization has set itself. It is useful to appreciate that current reality is a moment poised between the past – stretching back through the history of the organization, and the future – what is to follow. Some organizations see their future as a continuation of their past, and invest considerable energy in *steady state* and *more of the same* management. Others recognize that history and tradition are no guarantees of survival, as many of our once great manufacturing enterprises have discovered. Increasingly, the orienting questions that managers ask will need to have a future-focused edge to them:

- What sort of future are we likely to find ourselves in?
- What will be the consequences of a business-as-usual approach to this future?
- In what particular ways will we need to adapt and change if we are to create a successful place in this future?
- What might we need to start doing now if we are going to be well placed to survive and thrive in this future?

A more deliberate future-oriented focus is vitally important if the management of change is to be more than simply a reaction to altered circumstances. Management needs to develop an acute anticipatory element too. This means that we have to be constantly adjusting our time perspectives (Figure 2.3).

*Figure 2.3* Time perspectives

In earlier times, change and development projects had longer shelf-lives, and the present seemed long enough to allow generous planning and implementation phases. Today, the present more quickly becomes the past, and the future has a habit of appearing long before we are ready for it. Management is no longer a a matter of bringing an organization back on to a previously devised course. New environmental factors, changing requirements, altered demands, novel situations and unpredictable events also have to be considered. In a turbulent educational environment the management of schools takes on an altogether more complex and hazardous quality. Success in the modern age is more a case of adapting to meet changed circumstances when they arrive, than taking note of changed circumstances and then setting up a change and development project in order to bring the school up to date.

One of the keys to this new form of organizational metabolism is learning – the capacity to know how to adapt in anticipation of change. Bob Garratt (1987) has suggested that a model formulated by Reg Revans twenty years ago has increased relevance today.

*Box 2.7*
*Organizational learning*
(Revans, 1980)
Revans said that for an organization to survive, its rate of learning must be equal to, or greater than, the rate of change in the external environment. He expressed this as:

$$L \geqslant C$$

Learning in this context is not the same as training or acquiring new knowledge. It is much more about awareness of and sensitivity to change. It involves scanning the environment for early signs of trends and tendencies, it requires an increased capacity to envisage possible scenarios and to formulate the likely consequences of one course of action over another. Perhaps more than anything else it requires a quality of imagination likely to have been sufficiently developed during our formal education.

- In what specific ways do you identify the need for development in your own areas of responsibility?
- What are your views on the relationship between objective and subjective phenomena in management?
- How specifically does your school demonstrate a capacity to learn at least as fast as the rate of change in the external environment?

## A model for development

A vital part of management work is the ability to understand the factors that are currently affecting a school, department or individual member of staff. Organizations – even small ones like a village primary school or a subject department in a secondary school – are exceedingly complex and it is not easy to identify all the variables affecting a situation. In order to facilitate the process of enquiry and explanation it is useful to employ some form of analytical framework. The model in Figure 2.4 is an expanded version of the Practice link in the 4P development chain described earlier in the chapter.

The model offers a way of structuring enquiry into the current state of an organization. It attempts to capture the dimensions of organizational life and their pattern of relationships by isolating three particular clusters of variables, each with its own set of management challenges.

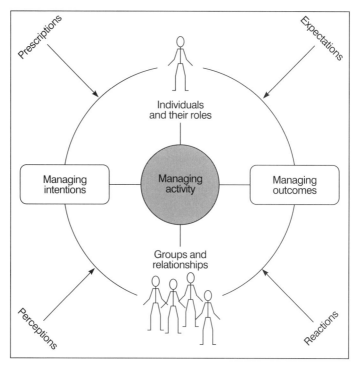

*Figure 2.4* A model of organizational life

1 *Boundary management* dealing with four distinct types of external pressure: prescriptions, expectations, perceptions and reactions.
2 *Strategic management* dealing with the management of intentions, activities and outcomes.
3 *Cultural management* dealing with the experiences and relationships of school members.

## Boundary management

Schooling is an essential part of social policy, providing a structured way of organizing the formal education of the nation's children. The structure conceived by the 1944 Education Act was of an education system centrally directed and locally administered. In practice the active partners in this process have been the schools and their local education authorities. During recent years we have seen a somewhat hasty disintegration of this established pattern, with central government taking a more controlling central direction while at the same time shifting the management focus from the local authorities to the schools themselves. A restructured definition of authority, with increased responsibility to governing bodies has created some confusion about the powers and duties among the various management partners. The

*Box 2.8*
*Boundary management*

*Prescription*
These are the forces which schools *must* attend to. For example:

- educational legislation
- welfare legislation
- health and safety legislation
- regulations
- LEA requirements.

*Expectations*
These do not have the force of law but are equally influential in determining how schools are managed. They operate through moral authority – raising expectations as to how schools *should* be run.

*Perceptions*
In a climate of constant change the capacity for misunderstanding about how schools operate is high. A good deal of management work is a public relations exercise to minimize confusion and uncertainty.

*Reactions*
A great deal of time each day in schools is taken up with dealing with queries, requests for information, approaches by contractors, complaints from neighbours, interventions by welfare agencies, contacts with the police and visits from officials and advisers.

creation of grant maintained schools and city technology colleges has brought about a fragmentation of the somewhat monolithic schooling system that had previously prevailed.

Sensitivity to the external environment is a key consideration for all organizations. In commercial businesses, competitive edge is vital to survival. For schools, the sustaining of confidence and credibility is the essential element, creating the need for effective public relations and high-quality accountability. Schools need to be alert to subtle changes in the climate of local opinion and ready to respond to fluctuations in expectation and concern.

Boundary management is becoming an increasing feature of all professional roles in schools and is no longer the domain of the most senior managers.

> *Boundary management*
> - What are the prescriptive forces currently acting on the school? How are these received, communicated and dealt with inside the school?
> - What range of expectations are acting to condition the working of the school? How are these taken account of and related to the school's own expectations of itself?
> - How does the school see itself responding to an accelerating rate of change? In what ways is it learning to adapt to new circumstances?

## Strategic management

Strategy is the means by which an organization activates its purposes and intentions through practice to produce desired results.

---

*Box 2.9*
*Strategic management*

*Managing intentions*
Purpose is the first of the three strategic processes required to enable an organization to function effectively. One of the keys to organizational success is the ability of all participants to define and articulate clearly both the purposes for the specific role they occupy and the goals and objectives for the organization as a whole.

*Managing activity*
The second strategic process is concerned with action, the transferring of intentions and plans into a range of appropriate tasks and activities. If visions are to be achieved and intentions fulfilled, then enabling structures have to be created and developed. Management and leadership activities in this dimension are concerned with the effective co-ordination of resources, particularly human ones, in order to achieve consistently high-quality results and outcomes.

*Managing outcomes*
The third strategic process is concerned with assessing outcomes and end results. The productive school is one that succeeds in bringing about purposeful and planned change in its participants. The quality of management and leadership is judged on results rather than intentions.

---

> *Strategic management*
> ● What purposes does the school exist to serve?
> ● What visions of the future are held by individuals and by the staff as a whole?
> ● How are visions and plans arrived at, agreed between all those concerned and shared with all those involved?
> ● What are the essential practices of the school?
> ● How are the structures, procedures and systems related to the planned intentions?
> ● How are tasks and activities defined and shared?
> ● In what ways is commitment to the process of review demonstrated?
> ● What procedures for measuring product, performance and progress are there?
> ● How are these related to plans? How are results fed back to those involved?

### Culture management

Culture is that vital aspect of organization to do with the ways in which individual participants in organizational life, both individually and collectively work to serve planned objectives and create achievements. Figure 2.4 emphasizes the contribution to practice and action made by the two key elements of organizational culture – individuals and groups (Box 2.10).

> *Box 2.10*
> *Cultural management*
>
> *Individuals and their roles*
> In the search for management processes which are truly integrating and collaborative, it is vital to remember that all organizations are made up of unique and distinct individuals. A proper respect for individualism is a characteristic of an effective management culture and the leadership challenge is all about the harnessing of different patterns of knowledge, skills and qualities to the pursuit of organizational goals.
>
> The individual is the organization's most important resource. We need to strive to discover ever more effective ways of releasing the abilities and energies that are available within people and to create optimum conditions for personal and professional growth.

> *Groups and relationships*
> This dimension refers to that most vital aspect of organizational life – the way that people interact and relate to each other and the behaviours they display in the working environment. It includes the ways that values and attitudes are demonstrated, how issues of motivation are dealt with, how power and authority are exercised and how conflict is resolved.

The culture of an organization is invariably regarded as the outcome of people's behaviour. Developing culture and climate needs to be seen as an intention – the deliberate development of relationships, behaviours and values that are consistent with the declared vision. In this sense it is very much a strategic issue. Those in leadership positions need to recognize the central importance of organizational culture in their own management and leadership behaviour. Personal effectiveness in management roles is concerned with creating and developing the very best conditions to support the work of others so that they are encouraged to work to the optimum of their capability. It involves maintaining a psychological environment which is high in challenge but also ready with support. At the personal level, effective managers create for themselves appropriate work habits, an efficient work environment and pay attention to their own well-being and sense of fulfilment.

In schools, organizational culture is important at two levels. First, there is the management culture within which plans are made, decisions taken and the work of the school organized. Second, there is the culture of the classroom – the climate of values and behaviour which so affects the capacity of pupils to learn successfully. There needs to be comparability between the two. One of the most vital tasks for school leaders is to work at building and developing these two related cultures into a cohesive and interdependent climate of endeavour.

*Cultural management*
- How is life in the school experienced by its participants, both staff and pupils?
- In what ways is respect for individuality of experience and aspiration demonstrated?
- How does a concern for self-esteem show itself?
- In what ways do issues of organizational culture, climate and ethos form an explicit part of planned development, decision-making and professional development?
- In what ways can the school be considered to be a learning organization in terms of staff development?
- In what ways are staff encouraged to undertake teamwork and to develop the skills of collaborative management?

This model can be used for a variety of purposes and we shall be using it in further chapters of the book. The framework can be applied to a range of perspectives:

1 As a framework for whole school review.
2 As a model for whole-school planning.
3 As a guide to the strategic work of governors and staff.
4 To define roles and responsibilities.
5 To build programmes of professional development.
6 As a conceptual model of classroom life.
7 As a basis for curriculum planning.
8 As a guide to classroom organization.
9 As a personal planning framework.
10 By pupils to guide self-directed learning.

## The management review

Management work rarely takes place in a vacuum, disconnected from the past and future. It is usually a consequence of previous work and will undoubtedly affect what has to be done in the future. Figure 2.3 illustrated the time perspective which needs to guide our management work. What we do at the present moment develops and changes what has previously been done, and anticipates what is to come in the future. When the future arrives and is not all that we expected then further work is needed. Management decisions taken in the present inevitably become management problems in the future and virtually everything we do changes something that we previously thought was a solution to a problem at that time. The essence of management work is moving things forward in the light of changed and changing circumstances.

Planning and carrying out a management review enables us to acquire information that will help us to manage development and change effectively. In determining what we need to do to meet the needs of the future we need to understand what is happening in the present and to know what happened in the past.

The term 'review' has been chosen in preference to 'audit', since the latter term has strong connections with error-detecting investigations. While such a review will have an important place for measurement and assessment, it is essential to see the process as primarily concerned with achieving insight and deepening understanding. The current preoccupation with assessment and testing starts from a basic mistrust of schools to serve their pupils with purpose and integrity, and clings to the mechanistic world view of right and wrong, and rigid criteria. Organizations, particularly those committed to the human processes of growth and development like schools, are essentially messy and unpredictable, relating more to biological processes than to the hard and immutable world of traditional physics. Hard data alone will never be sufficient to provide the information we need to manage effectively.

There are two distinct but related purposes for conducting an organizational review:

1 To take stock of current activity in order to understand what is going on.
2 To be able use this information to inform decision-making about future activity.

Reviewing is the process that enables us to obtain the information, knowledge and understanding to make decisions and plans about future directions. To achieve this a number of discrete tasks are necessary:

● devising a framework for enquiry
● generating information
● analysing data
● drawing conclusions and making judgements
● taking decisions
● revising plans
● circulating reports.

While the tradition of organizational inspection is built on the principle that external assessors are best placed to review objectively, the understanding that matters most in the development of a school is that created by those who participate in it – the staff, pupils and parents. Independent views can be of enormous value in reaching this understanding, especially where the external specialists and the internal participants work together to common purposes in a spirit of collaborative enquiry. The long tradition in the business world of engaging skilled consultants to assist in organizational reviews would be of enormous benefit to schools, and could well replace the costly and cumbersome inspectorial system currently causing schools to proceed with so much caution and anxiety that they are in danger of halting urgently needed innovation and development altogether.

The review model offered here envisages a substantial management project, when, for example, a major problem has been identified, or when significant innovation is necessary. It is also appropriate when a new post holder needs to take stock in preparation for the challenges ahead. The model can also be used in the process of continuous monitoring that is involved in most management roles in schools and can act as a useful checklist for almost any sort of management task, offering a systematic approach to the gathering of information.

Designing an organizational review presents a major challenge – how to manage the tricky relationship between objective and subjective reality. For some, a preoccupation with logic and rationality demands that attention be given only to objective phenomena – hard, measurable data and the use of predetermined performance indicators. Others, recognizing that organizations are made up of individuals with their different experiences, viewpoints and understandings, recognize the vital importance of paying attention to how people feel, what they think, what they aspire to, and the extent to which they are committed to corporate goals and shared ambitions. Undoubtedly an organization needs its hard data if it is to survive, and successful organizations go to great pains to set up systems to measure and assess those parts of organizational life that are appropriate to such devices. But they also recognize the crucial need to look below the surface reality of facts and figures to the more elusive and intricate human process that create them.

The question is not whether to pursue either objective or subjective factors. An organizational review exercise is concerned with both, and those involved in the review process will need to be aware of the distinction between the two – the methods that best suit each, and the extent to which the information that is generated is useful in enabling the organization to make appropriate decisions about its future.

## Review design

In preparing to undertake a management review it is helpful to use the 4P chain:

*Purpose*
● Why do we need a review?
● What do we need to know about?

---

*Box 2.11*
*Purpose and product*
A useful way to determine purpose or purposes for a review is to write down the sentence which begins:

> *I am going to carry out a*
> *management review in order to . . .*

and then complete the sentence with as many purposes as seem relevant.

Similarly some clear idea of the product can be gained by completing the sentence:

> *What I will end up with when the*
> *review is finished is . . .*

---

*Policy*
● What review systems are we currently committed to?
*Practice*
● How will we conduct the review?
● Who will be involved?
● How long will it take?
*Product*
● With what sort of data and information do we want to end up?

The practice stage is somewhat more involved and can be considered as a sequence of discrete activities (Figure 2.5).

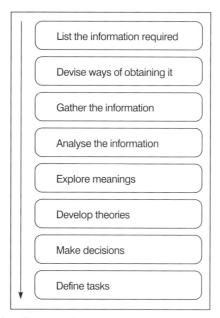

*Figure 2.5*  A review framework

### List the information required

The quality of a review and its subsequent activities is largely determined at this stage. Much will depend upon the purposes set, whether the enquiry relates more to the search for general understanding or to attain precise indications of performance in specific areas. Various kinds of information might be required:

● statistics
● records
● reports
● observations
● experiences
● opinions.

### Devise ways of obtaining the information

There are three basic ways that information can be obtained – documentary sources, personal observation and interpersonal enquiry. Methods might include:

- reading documents
- carrying out observations
- listening to what people say
- asking questions
- exploratory dialogue
- questionnaires.

### Gather the information

It is usually wise to inform people that a management review is being planned and to invite positive co-operation with it. This is where the purpose, policy and product links in the development chain can be so useful. People will want to know why a review is being organized and what will happen to the results. It is good practice to circulate the plan and to indicate the review timetable. It is also important to note that the very process of carrying out a structured review also affects the behaviour of the organization. The uncertainty principle formulated by Werner Heisenberg (1971) suggests that the act of observation changes that which is observed, and that the more scientific we become in trying to measure, the less we will see of the phenomenon we want to study.

### Analyse information

What we will usually acquire is some factual data and a range of personal thoughts, feelings and experiences. The skill in analysis is to be clear about the difference between fact and opinion, but not to underestimate the value of the latter. In a complex, intensely human organization like a school, it is the subjective data that cannot afford to be ignored. How people think and feel about what they do and how well they are doing it is as important as objective indicators of performance. In the end it is through people's thoughts and feelings that change is managed.

### Explore meanings

Data can be quite easy to produce. Deciding what it means can be a much more hazardous affair. It is easy for a government to suggest that crime is on the decrease according to official statistics, when in fact fewer people are reporting criminal incidents because so little seems to be done about them. An improvement in examination results could be the result of easier examinations rather than an improvement in learning. General systems theory can help us here with its emphasis on the need to study not only the data itself, but the relationships between the different factors producing the data.

Piecing together all the various bits of information into a clear and accurate picture is one of the most crucial skills of management. Professional judgement will need to be applied to the mixture of facts, opinions and impressions. We take on management roles because we are good at this, but we must remember that judgements arrived at are not the same as truth, they are inevitably our own opinions applied to the various items of information at our disposal.

### Develop theories

At this stage we can begin to look at the options available to us. If the analysis seems to indicate that change, development and improvement are necessary, then possible lines of action need to be considered. Good managers think very carefully at this stage, knowing that there are no simple solutions to the complex problems that occur in schools. Scenario-building is a useful tool – requiring us to consider the implications of different actions on those involved in implementing them, and on the nature and quality of the end result. This will involve the consideration of costs and benefits and the difficult and sometimes awkward balancing acts that this sometimes requires.

### Make decisions

Making a decision about what to do is also an act of professional judgement involving a complex synthesis of factors. It is here that the purpose link in the development chain becomes so important – will this particular course of action satisfy the purposes and values established within the school?

### Defining tasks

The general purpose of review is to determine what needs to be done. Once the decision is made it is tempting to think that the task is finished. A great many innovations fail because the hard and painstaking work ceases once a decision has been made. So far in the sequence we have been dealing with possibilities, now we have to make things happen.

One way to approach the evolutionary crisis in management with its attendant ambiguities, uncertainties and confusions is to try to minimize the huge potential for misunderstanding in most organizations. We need to be much more careful about the way we communicate meanings and decisions to those we work with and those who look to us for effective leadership.

Far too often development tasks are defined in vague and casual ways:

- Improve reading standards.
- Introduce group work.
- Develop the use of computers.

The trouble with these as task definitions is that while they identify a focus – reading, group work and computers – they fail to create any clear picture of what those involved in managing the change will actually need to do. The verbs are too general and passive. Language is central to effective management in complex times. We need to move away from the vague generalities that many change programmes are defined by, and seek tighter and more active styles of expression. For example:

- Devise a range of methods to improve reading standards in Year 5 by the end of the academic year.
- Design a programme to encourage Year 7 pupils to use group-focused learning in humanities subjects.
- List a range of ways that computer-assisted learning would benefit pupils in science.

Since a great deal of management work is conducted in short stints of time it is vital to see complex tasks as requiring a series of sub-tasks, clearly defined and specified. We can no longer afford the luxury of vagueness, it can be a major cause of procrastination and task helplessness. If, under pressure, we are not sure what we should be doing about a particular thing it is likely we will do something else instead, and so complex projects get delayed through misunderstanding and a shortage of clarity.

The model outlined in Figure 2.4 suggests three distinct types of review:

- *Boundary review*  An examination of how the relationships between the school and its external environment are managed.
- *Strategic review*  An examination of the systems and structures of the school and how well they are operating.
- *Cultural review*  An examination of the individual experiences, the interpersonal dynamics and the collective behaviour of the participants in school life.

Within this threefold classification questions can be raised to cover most aspects of school life, the answers to which will provide essential information about the organization, its people, its modes of operation and its perceived effectiveness.

- What are your experiences of taking part in major review exercises? What have you learnt from them?
- How do you manage the monitoring and review aspects of your own role?
- In what ways can we encourage the development of a powerful review consciousness in schools?
- What are your views about the current assessment and inspection procedures?

# 3 Visions and intentions

Here the starting point was critical: a broad vision seemed more likely to generate movement than a blueprint. Such broad visions were found to have significant process and implementation benefits in terms of commitment building and allowing interest groups to buy into the change process . . .
(Pettigrew)

## Introduction

In a world plagued with pressure, complexity and confusion it is ever more important to create visions of where we want to go, both in our personal lives and in our professional ones. We also need to develop ideas about the routes we will need to take to reach these destinations. The production of school development plans has become something of an obsession in recent years, yet it is the process of planning itself which is more important. Perhaps too often the documents simply occupy space in an already overloaded filing cabinet.

This chapter will focus on the management work involved in formulating visions and intentions for a school. In particular it will:

- outline the processes involved in strategic management
- examine the directional tendency in people
- consider the need for a future focus in leadership and management work
- distinguish between organizational and personal visions
- explore issues of leadership and vision-building.

---

- What are your own professional visions for your school, in your current role and for your career?
- What sort of vision do you have for education in the future, say, by the year 2010?
- Which of your visions do you feel you are nearest to realizing?

# Strategic management

Strategy is a key concept in the theory and practice of management and occupies a central place in the literature. It has been defined as having two key aspects (Johnson and Scholes 1989):

1 Matching the activities of an organization to its environment.
2 Matching the organization's activities to its resource capability.

Strategy involves a wide range of considerations:

- the environmental forces operating on the school
- the values and expectations of those involved in it
- the location of power and influence in the life of the school
- the resources available to managers
- the long-term direction of the school.

In these days of rapid and accelerating change it is also important to note that:

- Strategic decisions are often very complex in nature.
- They involve a high degree of uncertainty.
- They affect all those involved in the management of a school – staff and pupils.
- They are likely to involve change and innovation.

---

*Box 3.1*
*Strategic management*
(Johnson and Scholes, 1989)
Strategic management is concerned with deciding on strategy and planning how that strategy is to be put into effect.
   Strategic management has three main elements:

*Strategic analysis*
   Seeking to understand the strategic position of a school.
*Strategic choice*
   Formulating possible courses of action, their evaluation and the choice between them.
*Strategic implementation*
   Planning how the strategy can be put into effect.

---

With these three approaches in mind let us consider the strategic element of the management framework introduced in the previous chapter (Figure 3.1). This illustrates the three levels of strategic management outlined by Johnson and Scholes, and also the three

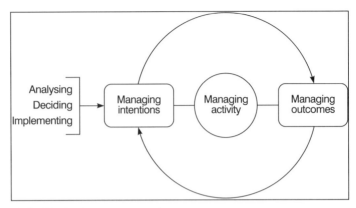

*Figure 3.1* Strategic management

phases highlighted in Figure 2.4 in Chapter 2. The strategic levels flow through each of the phases, producing a matrix of management activities (Figure 3.2).

The looped arrows in Figure 3.1 also remind us that planning involves the identification at the planning stage of desired end results, and that evaluation requires that we check outcomes with previous plans before we can make judgements about success and effectiveness.

| | Intentions | Activities | Outcomes |
|---|---|---|---|
| Strategic analysis | Analysing the needs of the school | Designing systems and structures for running the school | Analysing outcomes and results |
| Strategic choice | Formulating visions and intentions | Formulating specific tasks and activities and allocating roles | Making judgements about quality and effectiveness |
| Strategic implementation | Planning implementation projects and tasks | Leadership to support the management of tasks and activities | Defining and devising development projects and tasks |

*Figure 3.2* A matrix of strategic activities

This strategic framework applies to a great deal of management work in schools:

- whole-school strategic management
- departmental strategy (secondary)
- curriculum co-ordination (primary)
- subject leadership

- key stage and year management
- classroom management
- lesson management
- pupils' management of their own learning.

In many organizations, particularly large manufacturing ones, each stage of the strategic process would be managed by discrete groups of managers in separate departments – planning, operations and quality control. In schools, management processes tend to be more implicit and integrative. In the management of learning in classrooms, teachers need to be adept in each of the strategic phases and comfortable in the constant shifting that is required between each. Sometimes there is a complex simultaneity about the strategic process, with each of the elements relating to all of the others in a complex tapestry of factors and considerations.

In a world abounding with linguistic ambiguity it is important to attempt to define the terms we use in this important future-focused work. There are now a plethora of terms and phrases referring to the management of intentions – dreams, visions, mission, the big idea, global policy, strategic purpose, value statements, action plans, programmes, plans, targets, goals, aims and objectives. While there are no standard definitions to underwrite security of understanding, it is important to place these terms within some framework of meaning if management work is to be systematic and purposeful. For the purposes of this book the following working definitions are offered (Whitaker, 1997).

---

*Box 3.2*
*Managing intentions: terms and definitions*

*Visions*
Dream
    A glimpse of the future in which our life purposes and yearnings find fulfilment.
Vision
    A deliberately created mental picture of the future in terms of 'how we want it to be'.

*Policies*
Mission
    A deliberately stated intention to work towards specific aspects of this vision.
Policy
    A statement of commitment to a particular area of development.

*Plans*
Programme
   An outline of the development tasks to be accomplished in a given time.
Plan
   A detailed specification listing the action steps to accomplish the programme and serve the policy.
Aims and objectives
   Largely interchangeable terms for concrete and specific intentions within a particular action plan.
Goals and targets
   Largely interchangeable terms for concrete specifications for an end result.

This gives us three layers in the first strategic phase – visions, policies and plans.

Dreams and visions are both to do with our hopes and aspirations. Dreams capture what it is we really believe in and what we want to achieve for the pupils in our care, and for the teachers who carry the responsibility for managing their learning. Visions are more about what it will look like and sound like when we have achieved it. While the word 'vision' is useful to describe a school's idea of how it wants things to be, the concept also contains a powerful and motivating sense of direction.

*Box 3.3*
*Dreams and visions*
(Senge, 1990)
Visions that are truly shared take time to emerge. They grow as a by-product of interactions of individual visions. Experience suggests that visions that are genuinely shared require ongoing conversation where individuals not only feel free to express their dreams, but learn how to listen to each other's dreams. Out of this listening, new insights into what is possible gradually emerge.

It is through the many professional conversations each day that dreams and visions are built. As we listen to what our colleagues think and feel about the school and its future, and contribute our own thoughts and ideas connections are made and insights gained. As Senge (1990) says, powerful visions that are truly shared do take time to emerge.

*Box 3.4*
*The vision-led school*
(Simon, in Senge, 1990)
Traditional organizations change by reacting to events. The reason for this, I think, is that the 'reference points' for traditional organizations are external, outside ourselves. Usually these reference points are the way things were in the past. Sometimes they include the way our competitors operate. Change means giving up these reference points. So, naturally, it is resisted. To be vision led means that our reference points are internal, the visions of the future we will create, not what we were in the past of what our competitors are doing. Only when it is vision led will an organization embrace change.

The issue of the manager's role in the defining of purposes and intentions is a vital one. We have inherited the tradition that one of the key functions of managers is to define and articulate the purposes and intentions for those lower down in the organizational hierarchy. This was based on the assumption that only managers had the wisdom and experience to understand the aspirations of the organization, and that those lower placed would not be sufficiently interested or concerned in them to participate in their formation. Fortunately, such assumptions are only for the most unenlightened organizations these days, and it is now a central tenet of modern management theory that all those involved in the organizational enterprise need to be involved in the formulation of visions and intentions.

In schools, however, the tradition has tended to find the headteacher as the formulator and guardian of vision. A key feature of the headteacher selection process is likely to have been an examination of each candidate's vision for the future of the school. For some heads this can be too tempting to resist, and they see their role as requiring staff to commit themselves to the vision which was endorsed through the appointment process. Other newly appointed heads, anxious to introduce a more participative and collaborative management ethos into the school, sometimes find that the forces of tradition have created a tendency for staff to imagine themselves more secure when they are told what to do.

*Box 3.5*
*The Moses tendency*
(Anthony, 1994)
The leader becomes the opposite of the sacrificial goat that carries all sin. The leader is the visionary who has talked with God and who descends the mountain carrying the law.

We will examine the leadership implications of this dilemma in a later chapter but it is important to recognize that a school is not a command structure in which everyone is required to do as they are told, but a complex professional organization requiring the most skilful synthesis of capability and commitment. When too much expectation is placed on the head or any other single manager, then there is danger.

The complexities of present circumstances should discourage such a messianic approach to the management of schools.

---

- Use the various strategic models presented in this section to reflect on and analyse your own role. What do you find?
- Consider the terms and definitions outlined in Box 3.2. To what extent does the planning process in your school take account of the three layers?
- How are the visions for the future of your school determined? How are pupils encouraged to share the various visions and dreams?

---

## The directional tendency

The notion that people at work have to be separated into two groups – those who manage and those who are managed – has failed to take account of a significant psychological aspect of the human condition. The concept of a directional tendency in people suggests that living is a process of becoming – a gradual unfolding of personhood. Leading humanistic psychologists such as Abraham Maslow (1978) and Carl Rogers (1980) have argued that individuals have within themselves vast resources for healthy and successful living. These resources can become minimalized and suppressed during the long process of childhood socialization, but can be rekindled if a supportive psychological climate is created. Such an actualizing tendency is a characteristic of human beings but is also present in all organisms.

Traditional styles of management have tended to reinforce the suppression of potential, and senior staff in organizations have tended not to concern themselves deliberately with building the psychological climate in which this directional tendency can be promoted. As leaders, we need to consider to what extent the current culture and climate of our organizations provide conditions conducive to human growth and development, and the extent to which supposed underperformance can be attributed to the undernourishing quality of the human environment.

Successful leadership is very much a process of activating potential and of providing the space and conditions in which it can be creatively expressed. A key aim for leaders is the cultivation of the actualizing tendency in themselves and in each and every member of staff. This emphasizes the processes of releasing and empowering, rather than those of controlling and supervising – for so long the prevailing behaviour of those in authority roles.

---

*Box 3.6*
*The directional tendency*
There is in every organism, at whatever level, an underlying flow of movement towards constructive fulfilment of its inherent possibilities.

> . . . individuals have within themselves vast resources for self-understanding, for altering their self concept, their attitudes, and their self directed behaviour – and that these resources can be tapped if only a definable climate of facilitative psychological attitudes can be provided. (Carl Rogers, 1980)

Abraham Maslow (1978) used the phrase the 'actualizing tendency' to describe the directional tendency. He describes the type of people in whom this directional tendency is particularly strong and noticeable to their friends and associates:

> Self actualizing people are, without one single exception, involved in a cause outside their own skin, in something outside of themselves. They are devoted, working at something, something which is very precious to them – some calling or vocation in the old sense, the priestly sense. They are working at something which fate has called them to somehow and which they work at and which they love, so that the work–joy dichotomy in them disappears.

---

What these facilitative psychological attitudes and behaviours are we will explore in later chapters. What is important for the moment is the idea that we are all born with a powerful capacity to strive towards the fulfilment of our enormous and innate talents and capacities. One of the major paradoxes of human life is that given these enormous personal resources, so much is done in society to thwart them. The tragedy for most of us is that we ourselves have come to believe in our own modesty, the truth of our own incapacities and the limitations to our own development.

One of the key purposes of organizational leadership is to serve this powerful tendency, to awaken it and help to direct it creatively with intense sensitivity towards the realization of personally held organizational goals.

It is the identification of the cause which is so important, and which so much of life's experience conspires to obscure. We each have a cause, but few of us believe we do, and it is the purpose of life to unfold the cause by every means at our disposal. Leadership needs to become a mission to serve this process of unfolding in all those who come to work in schools.

---

*Box 3.7*
*The human resource*

We all bring into school a wholly unexplored, radically unpredictable identity. To educate is to unfold that identity – to unfold it with the utmost delicacy, recognizing that it is the most precious resource of our species, the true wealth of the human nation. (Roszak, 1981)

The essence of the human paradox referred to earlier is what Maslow (1978) describes as the Jonah Complex – that debilitating condition that promotes self-limitation and stunted development:

We fear our highest possibilities (as well as our lowest ones). We are generally afraid to become that which we can glimpse in our most perfect moments, under the most perfect conditions, under conditions of greatest courage. We enjoy and even thrill to the godlike possibilities we see in ourselves in such peak moments. And yet we simultaneously shiver with weakness, awe and fear before these very same possibilities.

---

One of the most important precepts of management and leadership work must be deliberate awareness of, and attention to, this directional tendency in those for whom we accept responsibility at work. Yet the history of management has been built on a thoroughly pessimistic view of human potential, as Chapter 1 has illustrated. Traditional orthodoxy has exploited certain aspects of human experience – economic necessity in particular, and has tended to regard people as expendable costs. What profligate waste of such a valuable resource. Unlike material resources – to which traditional orthodoxy has afforded almost reverential regard – people choose the amount of skill, energy and enthusiasm they release to any activity.

The directional tendency thus becomes a powerful reason why the formulating of visions and intentions needs to become a significant management activity, involving all participants in school life, pupils included. Succeeding in this depends upon each person feeling a powerful sense of identity with, and commitment to, the school's ambitions for the future. Vision-building and planning are not only functional activities designed to help a school move forward, they are the vital means by which all participants in school life build a share in the school and its future.

> ● What are your views of the directional tendency as outlined by Rogers and Maslow?
> ● What childhood experiences can you recall where you felt your emerging potential was thwarted? What was it like for you when your talents were recognized and encouraged?
> ● In what ways is the directional tendency encouraged and inhibited in your school?

## A sense of the future

One of the consequences of living at a time of rapid and accelerating change is that the future seems to arrive alarmingly early. As managers of schools we are faced with the challenge of preparing children for adult life in a future that we cannot predict with the same assurance that was once possible. Therefore we cannot be sure that what we teach them will be valid and useful in twenty or thirty years' time. Placing an emphasis on knowledge, much of which is likely to be irrelevant in a couple of decades or so, runs the risk of disabling learners who may have plenty of knowledge and information, but are living in a world where it is of little use to them.

Alvin Toffler (1971), writing about the disorienting nature of rapid change has suggested that the real beneficiaries of the educational system will be those who have acquired the skills of learning, rather than those who know a lot. It is the difference between capability intelligence and knowledge intelligence – between those who can adapt and those who cannot.

Since the process of rapid change imposes great challenges to forward thinking and long-term planning, there has developed an increasing emphasis on the need for skills in adaptation and change. Adaptation is not merely a reactive tendency, but a creative and imaginative process of relating development to emerging trends and tendencies, rather than only to current circumstances.

The lessons of history alone are unlikely to help in the future, since many of these emerging trends and tendencies are novel, posing challenges that have not been faced in any previous time and for which novel solutions will need to be found. This suggests that management and leadership work needs to acquire a more future-focused dynamic – a capacity to live with uncertainty but also to be alert to changes in the environment in which the school's work is set. We need to become adept at scanning the environment for signs of new ideas, developing trends and emerging possibilities.

In recent years, studying the future has become increasingly important as the world faces a whole range of political, ecological, technological, scientific and social challenges. Many who work in this field suggest that it is vital that we stop seeing the future as an inevitable consequence of the past and present, and ourselves as victims of it. The future is created by individuals and groups having visions in the present and doing something about them. While the *future* is often referred to in the debate about education, little thought seems to be given to its features and characteristics.

---

*Box 3.8*
*Categories of the future*
(Hicks and Holden, 1995)
*Tacit futures* – those which are implied but never clearly stated – e.g. the National Curriculum entitlement to preparation for adult life.
*Token futures* – more visible but only in a rhetorical way – e.g. 'education for the future'.
*Taken for granted futures* – the most visible of the three, a particular view of the future is proposed, but its virtues or likelihood are not questioned in any way.

For the future to feature as a more deliberate part of our thinking and planning, Hicks and Holden argue, we need to move beyond these limited perspectives. A futures dimension in school management involves an appreciation that there are *alternative futures.* What we need to do, they suggest, is to explore alternatives, to examine the values and assumptions behind different views of the future. In particular we should consider two further categories:

*Probable futures* – those which seem most likely to come about.
*Preference futures* – those which we feel ought to come about.

---

Those who are currently managing the schools of our country are faced with an awesome responsibility. The building of the future for schools has become increasingly centralized in recent years, and much of the decision-making for the way that schools manage the educational process has been removed from professional educators in schools and taken over by politicians and government agencies. The professional stake in education must not be sacrificed, and what happens to our schools in the years to come will depend very much on the stance that professional teachers take now and in the immediate years ahead. Teachers have their own powerful values and visions – that is why they have committed themselves as educators. A significant dimension for school management in the future will be determined by our capacity to envision the preferable educational futures we want for our children, and to work with passion and commitment within the current legislative boundaries to make them happen. Submitting to the inevitability of the probable future may well send us into another dark age from which it will be increasingly difficult to emerge.

> ● How do you envisage that schools can help pupils to develop a greater adaptive intelligence that will guide them through the twenty-first century?
> ● Define a probable future for the schooling system. What different elements would your preferable future have in it?
> ● What is your view about the current balance between government and professional direction in the management of schools?

## From visions to plans

The advent of faster change than we tend to be comfortable with poses a fascinating paradox. First, it is necessary to develop the capacity to be flexible and adaptable to fast-changing circumstances. But it is also necessary to proceed with integrity to principles and values. Vision is not simply a matter of knowing where you want to go, it is about the tantalizing issues of how you proceed into the future where confusion, uncertainty and turbulence have replaced the surer foundations that our predecessors once relied on.

Earlier in the chapter the management of intentions was defined as having three levels – vision, policy and plan.

### The vision

This is an internalized picture of how we would like things to be at some stage in the future. The vision is idealized, featuring desirable characteristics and successful activity. It is also highly motivating because the vision is what we believe in, what drives us forward in ambition and aspiration.

### The policy

This declares our commitment, announces what we offer and what we set out to achieve. It is a statement of intent others can use to judge us by.

### The plan

This is much more prosaic. It is written down as a set of steps into the future. It is realistic and practical, concerned with daily action towards identified targets. Plans tend not to have the inspiring ideals of the vision, nor the motivating commitments of policy. What they do contain are practical guidelines, precise goals and targets and a timetable for development.

Working simply to plans creates a management version of painting by numbers. We end up with a picture but with prepackaged colours and somebody else's drawing. It lacks those most vital of ingredients – artistic integrity and individual creativity. On the other hand, relying simply on a vision can leave too much to chance and increases the temptation to revise the vision when action fails to realize it.

What we have witnessed in the recent history of education has been an almost obsessive preoccupation with plans. The creation of targets that can be articulated without ambiguity and the measurement of attainment against them has become the dominating imperative of educational change. Nowhere has there been attention to the big ideas of education, the fundamental purposes in human development and aspiration that learning serves, only the dull and somewhat lifeless attention to detailed prescriptions.

Vision-building enables us to create and develop strong commitments to serve the principles and values of the school. The surest way to determine whether an organization has a vision is walk into it and ask the people who work there what the vision of the organization is. If they refer you to the executive suite or provide a series of inconsistent replies then clearly there is no cohesive and concerted effort to serve a set of agreed values and principles. But if you get clear and consistently similar responses about values and visions, you can be assured there is a sense of shared endeavour and a united effort towards organizational goals and targets.

## Organizational and personal visions

Vision-building and planning involves us in defining the sorts of organizational and personal futures we want to create, and specifying exactly how we can bring them about. But the pressures and the freneticism that now surround us demand constant attention to short-term expediency with scarce time to take account of longer-term plans and goals.

These conditions are quite unlike others experienced before in organizational history and require new conceptual frameworks as well as new practices. The notion of spans of change can help us to develop the sort of professional metabolism necessary to cope effectively in these novel and constantly changing conditions. Four main time spans can be considered (Figure 3.3).

Such a framework can help us to adjust our thinking to various spans of activity across the present – stretching back into the past and probing forward into the future. Increasingly we find ourselves

| Time span | Calculated in: |
|---|---|
| Long term<br>Medium term<br>Short term<br>Immediate term | years<br>weeks, months<br>days<br>hours, minutes, seconds |

*Figure 3.3* Spans of time

realizing that decisions made only a few months before have become problems in the altered circumstances of fast change. It is sobering and often frustrating to realize that decisions made about the future will be increasingly temporary and short term. While visions will set our principles and values for the long-term future, our plans will need to be seen as devices to take us a little way forward into the future.

We have tended to think of the past in terms of years distant from the present. Since the majority of work is increasingly focused on short-term and immediate considerations, the past might more meaningfully refer to the previous item on the agenda of a meeting we are currently attending, or a suggestion made in a professional interaction conducted only ten minutes before.

It is also useful to conceive of the four types of time span as having a key emphasis – long-term visions, medium-term strategy, short-term tactics and immediate choices and decisions (Figure 3.4). Effective management of time depends upon our ability to create a dynamic relationship between the four types of time span.

Personal and professional effectiveness involves working in harmony with this framework so that visions create purpose and a clear sense of direction for our work in the immediacy of the moment; and decisions and choices made in the moment-by-moment busyness of the working day result in helping the school move nearer to its vision of a better future.

| | |
|---|---|
| Visions | How we want things to be.<br>What we are all working towards. |
| Strategy | Current policies and plans to implement the vision. |
| Tactics | Ways to tackling the day-to-day work to meet the targets to realize the vision. |
| Choices | How we behave moment by moment in the tactical domain. |

*Figure 3.4* Categories of focus

Traditional orthodoxy has had much to say about organizational vision but little to say about the personal and individual visions of the staff who are responsible for realizing it. In the years ahead it will become increasingly vital to link the personal and the professional dimensions of our work. Successful organizations cannot be built on the assumption that our personal lives and their attendant issues and concerns can be left at the gate when we turn up for work each morning. The personal visions of staff are of acute concern to managers, since the probability of organizational success is enormously increased if we have a staff of achievers who are also fulfilled in their personal lives. One of the most important questions managers need to ask themselves is, how can I help each of my colleagues to achieve a sense of personal fulfilment and success in this organization? This is why appraisal targets are so vital, and why a personal dimension in the appraisal process is so necessary to professional development.

Organizational visions are of little use unless they are shared by those who carry out the work. For too long in the history of organizations it has been assumed that anyone below management level is unmotivated and merely compliant to organizational ambitions. Helping individuals to encompass personal aims with organizational purposes is one of the biggest challenges of leadership, and one of the most vital aspects of management. Every one of us has desires and hopes about our future, and virtually all of us are motivated by the desire to make our personal future better than the present. Work is a vital part of most people's life plan, in however vague a form this may exist, and nothing is likely to make people more effective in their work than a deep feeling that they are fulfilling important and valuable aspirations and ambitions. The paradigm shift in leadership and management is very much about moving on to this more life enhancing agenda, and seeing these aspirations and ambitions as the central element in the leadership process.

Effective schools of the future will take it as axiomatic that organizational visions will include the personal and career ambitions of every member of staff, however lowly their status may traditionally

Box 3.9
Creating new worlds
(Peters, 1988)
Managers must create new worlds. Such brave acts must begin with a vision that not only inspires, ennobles, empowers and challenges, but at the same time produces confidence enough to encourage people to take the day to day risks involved in testing and adapting and extending vision.

have been perceived. In a school this must, of course, involve the ambitions of the learners themselves, for too long excluded from the vision-making process.

Since all of us are motivated by self-interest – a key feature of the directional tendency referred to above – it makes sense to start with the assumption that unless we can achieve a high match between individual visions and organizational visions there will be little chance of everyone pulling in the same direction and achieving the goals so lovingly set by those in the most senior levels of the school.

Part of the transition to a new paradigm in management is the vitally needed shift in assumptions about the nature of work and its importance in the personal lives of people.

---

*Box 3.10*

*Simultaneous loose/tight properties*

In their study of successful organizations, Peters and Waterman (1982) discovered a phenomenon in highly achieving companies which they defined as simultaneous loose/tight properties.

Essentially a phenomenon of synthesis the essence of this idea is the coexistence of firm central direction and maximum individual autonomy.

Organizations that live by the loose/tight principles are on the one hand rigidly controlled, yet at the same time allow (indeed, insist on) autonomy, entrepreneurship, and innovation from the rank and file. They do this literally through belief in the directional tendency in all participants and through life-focused values, both of which most managers in less successful organizations avoid like the plague.

---

Relating this to school management the tight and rigid aspect is the determination to involve everyone in the building and defining of the purposes and values. The freedom aspect lies in the ability of each individual to make personal decisions about style and operation that will best enable that vision to be achieved. Many organizations do indeed operate this loose/tight phenomenon, but the other way round. They have a looseness and vagueness about values and direction – an absence of a built vision – but a rigidity in the way people are managed, with tightness around petty rules and regulations which managers enforce with relentless attention to duty.

It is perhaps only when personal visions and organizational visions become successfully integrated that the optimum conditions for organizational success are created. There is much new work to be done here as the shift to a more optimistic and life-enhancing work ethic is built. One thing is certain, the continuation of traditional work assumptions in a world of increasing pressure and fast change is a recipe for disaster. In the end, the single factor that has to be faced is one of trust. How can we build trust in a world which has placed so much store in suspicion? Only by encouraging management work of the highest quality, where courageous leaders work with patience and forebearance to build visions of the enriching organization and the culture in which it can be realized.

> - To what extent does your school value the individual visions of both staff and pupils?
> - What assumptions and attitudes underpin the vision building process in your school? How are people involved and encouraged to participate?
> - How does the loose/tight configuration outlined in Box 3.9 apply in your school? How does it affect your own role?

## Managing visions and intentions

In order to make the envisioning process more systematic, it is useful to conceive of two distinct elements – task and process:

- *Task visions*  These focus on what it is that the school wants to accomplish. They will include the purposes and principles which define why the school was established, the policies and practices laid down to bring about these achievements and the goals and targets which provide the focus for the work of individuals.
- *Process visions*  These are concerned with the ways in which the work of individuals and groups are co-ordinated to bring about the desired outcomes. Process visions encompass beliefs about how people should be treated in the school, how line management operates, how people can be helped to work to the optimum of their skills and capabilities and how relationships should be managed in order to achieve targets and goals in ways which bring a sense of satisfaction and achievement to all those involved. In planning for process it is important to take account of all those factors which are likely to increase or decrease people's capacities to give of their best.

### Roles and responsibilities

To achieve optimum cohesion there needs to be clarity about roles and responsibilities. Each member of the staff team needs to feel that their role as defined takes account of:

- *Quantity*　The size of the role and the extent to which it o
  challenges appropriate to experience, salary level and capability.
- *Breadth*　The range of different responsibilities involved and the
  extent to which these can be managed within the time available
  without prejudicing each separate one.
- *Depth*　The intensity of the responsibilities and their feasibility within
  the resource provision available.

## Circumstances and resources

Process management also involves achieving a realistic relationship
between the aims and aspirations set for individuals and groups, and
the circumstances and resources of the organization. In building a
process vision it is essential to consider:

- *Finance and materials*　Individuals should not expected to reach
  impossible targets with insufficient funding and inadequate
  resourcing.
- *Time and opportunity*　Time should be allocated on the same basis
  as other resources, so that targets set are realistic and appropriate to
  time allowed.
- *Culture and climate*　The organizational culture should be such that
  individuals are sufficiently supported and challenged, but not treated
  unfairly and overloaded.

## Support and maintenance

Creating a management culture characterized by high-quality support
is vital in an organization as complex as a school and it is important to
consider how a range of quite specific individual needs can be catered
for:

- *Information*　Providing information relevant to the effective discharge of roles and responsibilities. Lack of information can cause
  enormous resentment and frustration when people feel that their
  efforts are being hindered by lack of information and interpersonal
  contact with colleagues about the work itself.
- *Confirmation*　Providing confirmatory feedback to individuals about
  their complex roles and responsibilities so that they know that their
  contributions are noticed and taken account of.
- *Affirmation*　Providing affirmatory feedback so that individuals are
  helped to develop a confident awareness of those areas of their work
  which are particularly valued and appreciated.

Confident capability is created in staff when there is both clarity and
comfort about these process factors. A great deal of individual stress
and organizational depression can be caused when people feel unclear

ut what is expected of them, when their work is unappreciated and
ored, when their authority is overridden, and when their own
mpts to change the nature of their work circumstances is denied
thwarted.

ouch bifocal vision is necessary to maintain an appropriate balance
between the purposes for people's work and the management
processes established to enable it to be conducted effectively.

> - How do the management processes in your school take
>   account of the task/process distinction?
> - Consider current management practice in your school in
>   relation to:
>   - roles and responsibilities
>   - circumstances and resources
>   - support and maintenance.
> - Analyse your own role in terms of task management and
>   personal support for others.

## Leadership and vision

Perhaps the most significant challenge presented by the process of
building an organizational vision for a school lies in the traditional
assumptions about how organizational direction and decision-making
is best managed. The view tends to be that it is the leaders who have
vision and the followers who need to be inspired to fall into line
behind it.

Behind recent trends towards staff participation and involvement in
decision-making has been the belief that such involvement increases
commitment among staff to organizational goals. This is a somewhat
simplistic view which can underestimate the motivational patterns of
people and their capacity to give themselves to causes that are not
always in their own best interests. Far too often *compliance* with
management is mistaken for *commitment*, but the two are very
different.

The idea of an *official vision* for a school is a contradiction in terms.
We have already defined vision as an internalized and highly
motivating picture of how we really want things to be in the
organization. This means that a vision, however articulated, needs to
resonate with the individual aspirations and predilections of each
member of staff. This cannot be achieved without the active participation of all staff as vision builders. This does not mean that senior staff
are helpless in the process. Clearly they are accountable for the
boundaries and principles which give the organization its existence. It
is senior staff who are responsible for explaining contractual obliga-

tions and the nature of governance. It is also a necessary function of senior staff to set the agenda for vision-building and to create the conditions within which all members of staff can bring their own ideas about how the school should develop.

One of the difficulties created by an excessive zeal about the value of documented planning is what can be described as the manifesto syndrome. At election time each political party produces a substantial manifesto containing all the detailed policies the party would pursue if elected to government. But only a very tiny proportion of the electorate who will be affected by these policies reads the manifesto. What happens is that abbreviated versions, articulated in headline form are produced and these become the rallying point. Schools have unwillingly tended to become slaves to the same syndrome, produced excessively detailed annual plans which when completed hardly anyone will ever read again. What is needed is something of more practical value, in other words a reference point for specific task and project plans – those created by individuals to guide their practical work in the weeks and months ahead. Such plans need to be:

● clear
● concise
● a signpost to the future
● a rallying point for commitment.

Far too many school development plans serve only an accountability purpose, and are produced because they are required by the bureaucratic process. Far better to create a culture where everyone is an inveterate visionary, forecaster, planner and programmer.

---

Box 3.11
*Leadership and vision*
(Bennis, 1989)
Effective leadership is the capacity to create a compelling vision and translate it into action and sustain it.

---

The leadership required to bring all participants into active collaboration in the vision-building process involves four key abilities:

● managing attention
● managing meaning
● managing trust
● managing self.

1 *Managing attention*   Leaders need to be vision focused. In their encounters with colleagues they should never miss an opportunity to link individual activities and achievements with the declared visions of the school. The bridge to the future is built when people come together to create and adopt a vision as their own, one that they can believe in and will strive for.

2 *Managing meaning*   Leadership is also about constructing, through dialogue and conversation, insights and understandings into the complexities of the process, so that each individual is helped to grasp the meaning of their own roles and responsibilities in relation to the visions and intentions of the school.

3 *Managing trust*   Trust is that elusive quality so vital to any enterprise built on shared endeavour. Leaders need to ensure that all those involved in serving the purposes of the organization feel they are trusted with the stewardship of its vision.

4 *Managing self*   There is a need for everyone to see their responsibility as collaborating in the creation of a powerful shared vision for the school. Leaders need to be good at activating the pursuit of awareness, persistence and self-knowledge in their colleagues. This involves a commitment by everyone to the process of continuous professional learning.

Good leadership is the guardianship of a shared dream. It involves the fostering of big ideas and bold ambitions. It is relentless in its determination to create both a big picture of the way things will be, but also to help generate the more detailed plans and programmes upon which quality and effectiveness will ultimately depend.

- How do you see your leadership role in relation to the building of a vision for your school?
- In what ways can visions be built so that they are compelling and motivating?
- Reflect on your leadership work in terms of:
  - managing attention
  - managing meaning
  - managing trust
  - managing self.

# 4 Getting things done

This new form of leadership fully understands the need for a step-wise process of change, and is willing to make the process explicit to all concerned. It takes the needs and aspirations of others into account at each step, and actively involves them in the endless task of learning from the experience of bringing about change. Above all, these leaders recognize the need to bring diverse points of view together, in vigorous encounter. In this form of leadership, learning grows from dialogue: from entering into the feelings and thoughts of others.
(Boot, Lawrence and Morris, 1994)

## Introduction

Getting things done is another way of describing the practice link in the 4P development chain and the central element in the strategic process outlined in Chapter 2. It is the means by which the purposes, visions and plans of the school are translated into action to achieve its ambitions.

The literature of strategic management is already substantial and is growing at an alarming rate as new theories and concepts vie for our attention. Early assumptions were based upon the idea that the necessary activities of an organization could be established by design, and that fixed structures could be devised which would ensure both efficiency and effectiveness. This may still be true in some industrial organizations which have have moved to computer-based robotic systems to manufacture their products, but there is now a growing recognition that we have significantly underestimated the human factor in our approach to the management of work.

The mechanistic assumption that has equated people with machines is being challenged. A new view is emerging, altogether more holistic, life focused and systems based. Not only does this view give greater attention to human behaviour in the organizational process, it emphasizes the essential connection and interdependence of all the contributory parts. In the face of necessity we are gradually coming to understand that people are not machines, and that strategic structures which operate in the belief that they are, will fail to realize and build on the enormous reservoir of commitment, skill and capability people have within them. Effective management is the challenge of releasing this reservoir in ways that bring deep satisfaction to the individuals involved, and high-quality benefits to the organization in which they work. And, so, it is to these human processes that we now turn.

The chapter focuses on the interpersonal world of management and leadership. In it we will:

- consider the interpersonal challenges involved in managing the work of others
- examine some of the complex dynamics involved in communication in schools
- outline the elements of interpersonal intelligence
- explore the interpersonal landscape of encounters and interactions
- discuss the interpersonal aspects of effective leadership.

## Managing human activity

In the management of human affairs, command and coercion have been necessary to create optimum control and order. As societies have embraced the democratic imperative it has been increasingly difficult to sustain the levels of order and organization that were once achieved by coercion, backed up by terrible punishments for deviation from established norms. Democracy is essentially a messy affair, requiring time and energy to operate effectively. Even in the late twentieth century, slavery continues to exist and many societies are still controlled by military tyrannies. In the early twentieth century, trade unions were necessary to speed up the shift from tyrannical exploitation of labour, and to force a radical rethink about how work can best be managed. While concepts of leadership and management are under review, and new and more life-enhancing approaches are spreading throughout the world of organizations, we can still feel ourselves in thrall to the hierarchical tendencies of the past with their unequal and oppressive distribution of power and authority.

In the movement from an essentially mechanistic approach to a more inclusive, humanistic and life-enhancing approach, it is necessary to change some of our traditional ways of thinking about how people should be treated at work. Rather than sweep the messiness of human affairs under the carpet it it necessary to regard it as one of the most significant aspects of organizational life, and to afford it the attention its complexity deserves. Small changes in personal moods, attitudes, emotional states and felt experiences can often have enormous consequences in an organization.

It is also important to realize that while the articulation of visions and goals can provide a rallying point for getting things done, much of the time our reasons for doing things emerge by chance and reflect the current dynamics of our constantly changing lives. The time has come to treat accidents as allies and to recognize the limited capacity we have to shape events in the ways we would like.

---

*Box 4.1*
*Messiness*
Perhaps it is the concept of messiness which now holds the most useful indication of what managers face in their attempts to create efficient and effective schools. Observing organizations at work will reveal a range of interesting phenomena:

- the richness of human experience contained within them
- the messiness of events and incidents that characterize most days
- uncertainty about tomorrow
- continual disorders despite our attempts at tidiness
- the fun and enjoyment that can sometimes be experienced
- the anguish and despair that is also felt
- varying levels of commitment, compliance and disruption.

---

Strategies, plans and performance indicators are small elements in such complexity and we must not be upset and surprised when the power of incidents and events cause our best laid plans to be overridden. Perhaps above all we need to learn that we cannot always manage by design, that there are usually more factors present than we are ever able to take account of.

What we need to be aware of is the reality gap between an envisioned world of perfection, with its clear concepts, well-articulated generalities, constant exhortations and big ideas, and the complex reality of unpredictable behaviour, countless incidents, confused experience and unexpected effects. The reality gap is the difference between the world we want, the one that is defined for us in our job descriptions, and the one we get, the one we encounter every day when we come to work.

- How do you view the changes in the management of work during this century?
- In what ways have your beliefs about how people should be managed at work changed during your lifetime?
- Reflect on the concept of messiness outlined in Box 4.1. How does this relate to your own view of how organizations work?

## Communication

Traditional concepts of management communication in organizations have been built on three key elements:

- clear instructions
- error feedback when things go wrong
- cajoling and exhortation.

The assumption of an endemic superiority of managers over those they manage has brought about the idea that workers need to be treated badly if they are to work at their best. If we are to change this harmful and counter-productive tradition, we need to look to the nature of the relationships we build with our colleagues, and to the language we employ when we interact with them. It is largely through verbal language that we convey our thoughts and ideas, and through non-verbal signals such as facial expression, bodily stance and tone of voice that we convey our feelings and emotions. Perhaps the majority of significant meanings we receive during any interpersonal interaction are non-verbal, conveyed through the expressions and gestures we use.

### The interpersonal landscape

Human communication is a hazardous business and the capacity for misunderstanding between people is enormous. It is a tribute to our natural and intuitive capacities that we can do it without more breakdowns, disagreements and conflicts.

---

*Box 4.2*
*Behaviour and experience*
R.D. Laing (1967) has suggested there is a vital distinction between behaviour and experience in interpersonal relationships.

- I can observe your behaviour. This behaviour then becomes an experience of mine.
- You can observe my behaviour which then becomes an experience of yours.
- I cannot observe your experience which is inside you, but I can try to understand your experience if you disclose it to me.
- You cannot observe my experience which is inside me, but you can try to understand my experience if I disclose it to you.

---

In the process of observing others – listening to what they say and watching what they do – we can begin to sense the nature of their experience. But we all have the capacity to dissemble – to say things and do things which are not congruent with what we are experiencing and feeling. This can lead to confusion, ambiguity, mixed messages and misunderstanding. To be more effective in our relationships we need to be aware of, and sensitive to, the complex nature of the interpersonal landscape between ourselves and others. It is important to note the range of intra-personal factors that combine to make us what we are and how we behave in different communication situations (Figure 4.1). Each of the factors referred to in Figure 4.1 affects how we think and feel, how we relate to others, how we manage ourselves and how we reach out into the world.

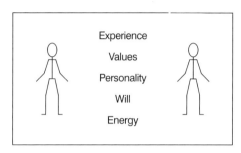

*Figure 4.1* The interpersonal landscape

## Experience

We each bring to our professional lives a unique set of experiences from childhood, our life in schools, in our relationships, at work and as members of society. We have been formed and moulded by these experiences and how we have responded to them.

## Values

Throughout our lives we have been developing attitudes, beliefs, assumptions and prejudices. While theses are rarely rigidly fixed some will be firmly held and will affect the decisions we make in our lives and the ways in which we communicate with those we meet.

## Personality

In addition to experience and values, our personalities are affected by our unique pattern of motivation – needs and aspirations – and how we strive to satisfy them. The strength of our self-concept will depend on how successful we feel ourselves to be in meeting the challenges we face in our lives. Those of us with an 'internal' locus of control are more able to make for ourselves decisions affecting our lives, whereas those of us with an 'external' locus will constantly seek the approval or permission of others to determine the direction of our lives. A further important factor is the extent to which we present ourselves to the world as we really are – with our fears, frustrations, anxieties, insecurities, guilts and fantasies – or as we would prefer others to think we are.

*Will*

> Our behaviour will depend on the ways in which our intentions are empowered into action, and the extent to which we experience an inner authority to serve our needs and aspirations. Without will and determination we are unlikely to make an impact in the social and professional worlds where relationships and communication are so vital.

*Energy*

> It is often our energy and enthusiasm which is most influential on others. Attempting to use rational argument without disclosing how we feel emotionally often fails to impress others. Sometimes our energy is contagious and others pick up on its intensity and quality. Approaching others when we feel apathetic or lethargic is likely to be counter productive,

## Experience and behaviour

> We have all been shaped and moulded by our experience. In any school each person has:

- grown up with family members who have provided powerful influences and presented models of behaviour
- acquired a personal history of communications and developed a unique profile of relationships
- developed a repertoire of strategies for interacting within our complex social world
- evolved a code of conduct to guide our actions in the world
- established a personal and distinctive set of habits and patterns.

A school is a complex organization in which a rich network of differentiated experience and belief is in a state of constant interaction. As well as the purely individual and personal elements, communication behaviour in an organization is affected by a variety of social and institutional structures:

- status
- authority
- power
- age
- race
- gender
- disability.

Each of these factors will further affect the ways in which individuals experience organizational life and how pecking orders, chains of command, informal networks and strategic alliances are established.

Over the last twenty years there have been concerted efforts to change oppressive communication cultures, particularly those built on

prejudices about age, race, class, gender and ability. Many organizations are careful to develop policies which protect individual groups
from exploitation and oppression. Central to these policies are issues of
interpersonal communication – the assumptions we make and the
language we use.

In most organizations communication is conducted in a climate of
increasing challenge and complexity as old assumptions are rejected
and new ones developed. It is important not to set standards so high
that people are discouraged from communicating through a fear of
making mistakes. An effective communication culture is one which
encourages development and expects a certain clumsiness as people
struggle to find new patterns and processes.

Building and developing relationships is a process of matching the
elements of our own unique world with those of others. The greater the
similarities, the greater the likelihood of an open and satisfying relationship. Most of the time our behaviour is purposeful, designed to meet
needs and satisfy aspirations. In comfortable relationships, where we
feel a positive sense of connection within the interpersonal landscape,
we tend to strive for harmony between our inner world and our behaviour – we become more open and trusting to the other person.

In difficult and uncomfortable relationships we experience a sense of
tension and dissonance in the interpersonal landscape. This can create
feelings of anxiety which can result in behaviour designed to protect
our inner world from attack and judgement – we become more closed
and defensive.

Clearly, the process of communicating is immensely complex and
there is a great deal to try and do in such a short time. We cannot plan
every communication incident in advance, since we do not know when
the majority of them are likely to arise, or exactly how the other person
will react and respond. But with those that we know we are going to
initiate we can try to take some of these important factors into
consideration as we prepare.

---

*Box 4.3*
*Improving communications*
As professional communicators we can be more prepared by:

1 Working constantly to increase our awareness
   ● of how we behave in interpersonal situations
   ● how the other person reacts and responds
   ● of the outcomes and effects of the encounter.
2 Developing strategies and behaviours which:
   ● increase our own effectiveness
   ● enable others to benefit from the encounter
   ● help the school to achieve its aims.

---

Communication is the the vehicle for management and leadership work. Without encounter there is no management. Interpersonal communication and its intricate complexities is the main curriculum for management development. Sadly it is the curriculum that is most neglected.

---

- Reflect on some recent interactions at work. Analyse them using the model formulated by R.D. Laing.
- Consider yourself in terms of the interpersonal landscape. In what ways do specific aspects of the five elements make you the person you are?
- Call to mind some good relationships at work. Which elements in the interpersonal landscape contribute to feelings of comfort and well-being?
- What about the more difficult relationships? Which elements contribute to your sense of discomfort?

---

## Interpersonal intelligence

The specific skills and qualities of interpersonal communication have not received much attention in the curriculum for schooling, and it is unlikely that they have featured very significantly in the professional training of teachers. Nor do they feature as significantly as they should in management training. Perhaps there is an assumption that if you are intelligent and well educated then you are automatically sensitive and skilful in the interpersonal domain. This is manifestly untrue as we all know from our personal experience.

In his work at Harvard University, Professor Howard Gardner (1993) has been developing a new concept of human intelligence, moving beyond the narrow and restrictive notions which have been used to judge human capability since the early days of the century. He places interpersonal intelligence with six others as the basis of a new concept of integrative and holistic intelligence (Box 4.4).

Gardner identifies four essential components of this interpersonal intelligence:

- *Social analysis* The skills discerning and understanding other people's feelings and concerns.
- *Personal connection* The process of reaching out to others and making contact at a deep interpersonal level.
- *Negotiating solutions* Communicating with others to prevent and inhibit conflicts and striving to resolve those that do flare up.
- *Organizing groups* Communicating with the group so as to express their unspoken collective sentiments and articulating shared goals and aspirations.

---

*Box 4.4*
*Multiple intelligences*
Gardner (1993) has identified seven intelligences:

- linguistic intelligence
- logical-mathematical intelligence
- spatial intelligence
- musical intelligence
- bodily-kinaesthetic intelligence
- interpersonal intelligence
- intrapersonal intelligence.

*Interpersonal intelligence*
The ability to understand other people: what motivates them, how they work, how to work co-operatively with them.

*Intrapersonal intelligence*
The capacity to understand and be aware of ourselves and to use these understandings and awarenesses to operate effectively in life.

---

This offers us four particular communicative roles:

- *Understander*   Using social analysis to understand the meanings in different people's experience.
- *Friend*   Making contact with colleagues and relating at a deep level of connection.
- *Mediator*   Working with others to iron out difficulties and frustrations and collaborating in the resolution of conflicts.
- *Leader*   Working with groups and teams to articulate shared experiences, identify collective needs and focus on goals and aspirations.

Interpersonal intelligence involves many skills and abilities often requiring us to search below the manifest and obvious in human communication behaviour to notice the invisible, listen for the inaudible and touch the intangible.

- Reflect on Howard Gardner's theory of multiple intelligences. What particular skills and capabilities contribute to intrapersonal intelligence and interpersonal intelligence?
- Use Gardner's four essential components to analyse and review your own communication style.
- How do the four communication roles – understander, friend, mediator and leader – relate to your own leadership and management work?

## Encounters and interactions

The essence of management work is conducting a never ending series of interactions with others. These will consist of two types of communication:

- *Casual communication*  These are the numerous situations when we encounter each other during the day, exchange pleasantries, remark about the current state of affairs or share observations. Although casual, they are very important in establishing and maintaining contact between colleagues, getting to know more about each other and tuning in to professional attitudes, aspirations and interests.
- *Significant communication*  These are communication incidents that are created to serve individual and specific purposes. We use them to resolve our own needs, to respond to the needs of others and to respond to planned arrangements. They are sometimes the outcome of scheduled meetings and at other times conducted when chance encounter permits.

Both types of communication are important. The extent to which the edges between the two are blurred or sharp says something about the quality of the organizational culture. In most effective organizations the brief exchanging of pleasantries is a useful prelude to the transacting of important business. It is important to realize that both forms have the potential to affect individuals as well as the school as a whole. A chance encounter can sometimes make or mar our day.

Our encounters and interactions will also fall into two categories (Figure 4.2):

- responsive interactions where we are approached by others
- initiating interactions where we approach others.

It is usually assumed that the initiating responses are the most important since these are part of our planned strategy – getting alongside colleagues and grappling with the big issues of the school. It is in this interactive mode that we are at our most proactive, carrying out work that we know has to be done and that we have prepared ourselves for. The responsive interactions can often be seen as interruptions to our proactive determination, deviating us from our prime purposes and setting back the work of the day.

If, however, we view these two different types of interaction in terms of the needs they satisfy, then we may develop a more helpful perspective. When others approach us, to seek advice of guidance, to ascertain a piece of information or to talk through a worry or concern, they are seeking support for a problem or issue which if not dealt with could involve significant reduction in their capability. By responding caringly and sensitively we can be releasing colleagues, pupils and

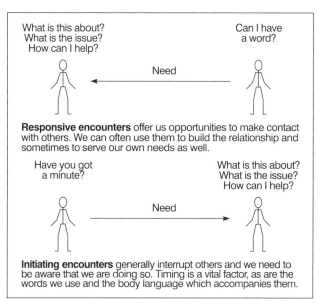

*Figure 4.2*   Initiating and responsive encounters

others from all sorts of temporary hindrances to the smooth management of their responsibilities, and creating a good deal of goodwill at
the same time.

When we deliberately approach others we do so because we have
identified a need which the other person may have the capacity to
satisfy. It is our need we are taking into the interaction, and ourselves
who are doing the interrupting. Leadership which is too regularly
intrusive and pestering is usually counter-productive. It is more
effective, where appropriate, to seize those reactive moments when we
have been approached by others to do some business of our own.

Approachability is a factor often referred to in organizations,
particular in relation to workers and their bosses. Verbal language and
body language are crucial in creating this approachability quality. Note
the different qualities about the following examples:

- Gentle enquiry: 'How was the course yesterday?'
- Specific request: 'Can you tell me . . .'
- Expression of need: 'I'm glad I've seen you. I would really value your
  help next week with . . .'
- Confronting the issue: 'Can we talk about that incident in the staff
  meeting last night?'

It is important in both these interactive modes to be aware of some
of the psychological dynamics that are set up. Each person, as they
approach the other with a view to engaging in communication sets

up what can be defined as interaction expectancy – the anticipating of what we would like to happen and what is likely to happen. If these two expectations are close together then we can be reasonably confident of our capacity to achieve what we want from the interaction. Figure 4.3 outlines the dynamics of interaction expectancy.

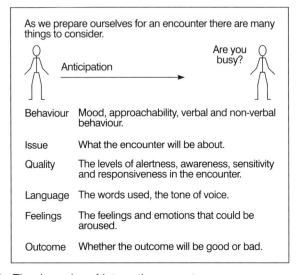

As we prepare ourselves for an encounter there are many things to consider.

Anticipation

Are you busy?

| Behaviour | Mood, approachability, verbal and non-verbal behaviour. |
| Issue | What the encounter will be about. |
| Quality | The levels of alertness, awareness, sensitivity and responsiveness in the encounter. |
| Language | The words used, the tone of voice. |
| Feelings | The feelings and emotions that could be aroused. |
| Outcome | Whether the outcome will be good or bad. |

*Figure 4.3*  The dynamics of interaction expectancy

Clearly a lot is going on in the hearts and minds of the two concerned. As these different intrapersonal and interpersonal elements combine, the interaction expectancy can form itself into a number of stances:

- Optimistic: 'This will be OK.'
- Pessimistic: 'This will be difficult/awkward.'
- Open: 'Let's see what happens.'
- Closed: 'Let's play it cool.'

Our individual patterns of anticipation will largely determine our capacity to:

- tackle new interactive situations
- resolve ongoing tussles
- manage uncertainty.

Our interactive history is likely to include a majority of interactions that have worked perfectly adequately, where business was done with a minimum of fuss with good feelings on both sides. Often we will have felt particularly poised and confident, enjoying our own verbal contributions and taking pleasure in those of the other person.

Our personal history will also include many difficult and awkward encounters, and some downright unpleasant ones too. In Figure 4.4 the concept of an encounter continuum is illustrated. It shows what happens when an interaction moves from relative ease and comfort to the more friendly level of warmth and enjoyment. It also shows the move from unconscious comfort to conscious discomfort, when we realize that the encounter is becoming difficult and awkward.

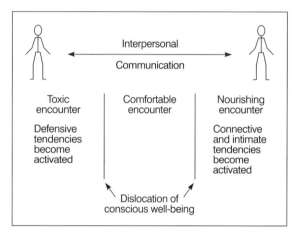

*Figure 4.4*   The encounter continuum

In the comfort zone, with both partners experiencing a sense of unconscious well-being, we are free to concentrate on the business in hand without having to transfer creative energy to keep the interaction going, or to deal with awkward responses. But sometimes a phrase, a tone of voice or a facial expression acts to heighten how we are experiencing the encounter, and we become conscious of feelings of surprise, anxiety or irritation. If this awkwardness is not quickly remedied, but is reinforced by other phrases, tones and expressions, then we experience a dislocation of comfortable well-being. If the small interactive elements have been particularly pleasurable and enjoyable then we may consciously begin to be aware of positive feelings and emotions, and our colleague is likely to pick these up. If the elements are unpleasant however, then we may consciously begin to feel anxiety, anger and frustration. When the dislocation is at the toxic end of the continuum then we have to search deep within our resources for more energy and creativity to try and bring the encounter back into the comfort zone.

In extreme cases, both kinds of dislocation can have devastating effects. Falling in love, like engaging in conflict, can inhibit our normal patterns of operating, fill us with intrusive thoughts, put us off our food and cause sleepless nights.

All types of encounter are common and inevitable, but we can work to push them through into the nourishing zone where increased energy and creativity are generated. Moving into the toxic zone is a common experience in management work and the loss of confidence and presence of anger and irritation can be very debilitating and challenging. It can begin to jeopardize the very task that we had set out to accomplish. When toxins intrude, it is vital to make our thoughts and feelings explicit, so that they can be appropriately managed and the difficulties dealt with. Those who are effective at tuning in to others' moods and working with them, rather than trying to avoid or ignore them, will more easily achieve smooth interactions at the emotional level.

Until quite recently the literature of leadership and management has taken insufficient account of these communication dynamics, and many managers find it frustrating that their new levels of authority are not automatically accompanied by an increased capacity to communicate effectively. Developing a curious fascination with the dynamics of human encounter is a prerequisite for effective leadership, for unless we are deeply interested in the inner landscapes of our colleagues' lives we are unlikely ever to know enough about them to be supportive, influential and inspiring.

---

*Box 4.5*
*The unconscious dance*
(Capra, 1996)
Film analyses have shown that every conversation involves a subtle and largely unconscious dance in which the detailed sequence of speech patterns is precisely synchronized not only with minute movements of the speaker's body but also with corresponding movements of the listener. Both partners are locked into this precisely synchronized sequence of rhythmic movements and the linguistic co-ordination of their mutually triggered gestures lasts as long as they remain involved in their conversation.

---

The purpose of communication is not only to transfer, convey and exchange information, but to connect at a deeply resonating level. It is often when two people's inner worlds resonate in harmony with each other that energy is created, insight gained, possibility increased and personal determination aroused.

---

*Box 4.6*
*Five ways of communicating*
The psychologist Virginia Satir (1982) says that she has only ever experienced five ways of communicating. These are:

- levelling
- distracting
- computing
- placating
- blaming.

She also declares a number of beliefs about the process of communicating:

- We are always communicating, our behaviour is always making a statement about us.
- Our communication is always purposeful.
- How we communicate limits how we perceive.
- I know better than you what I am trying to convey.
- You know better than me what I am conveying to you.
- By sharing our perceptions of each other's messages, we give both of us a chance to learn and understand.

---

There is much here to focus our management minds upon if we want to make a qualitative difference to our organization, and to get those things done that need to be done. Professional development for leaders is as much about the dynamics of daily interactions as it is about strategic frameworks, attainment targets and performance indicators.

Being open and honest does not mean that we always have to say things that others will find hurtful. It is often easier to deal with difficult situations by sharing what it is we are experiencing: 'Look, there is something I need to talk to you about but I am finding it very difficult and I'm afraid how you might react. I may not say it very clearly and I'm concerned that you may not understand.'

This may sound awkward and artificial, but this is because it is unfamiliar. Few of us have been lucky enough to witness the high quality levelling communication referred to by Virginia Satir (1982). We are much more familiar with verbal and non-verbal warfare. It actually pays to express our concerns both about ourselves and for the other person. We need practice in talking about our feelings in this way and in articulating our experience of the interaction itself. Effective school development involves a deliberate focus on the communication experiences of staff, and of the methods and techniques that can make for increased well-being and confidence.

> Call to mind a range of recent encounters and interactions at work. Review each of these in relation to:
>
> ● Initiating and responsive interactions – Figure 4.2.
> ● Interaction expectancy – Figure 4.3.
> ● The encounter continuum – Figure 4.4.
> ● The five ways of communicating – Box 4.4.

## Leadership

One useful definition of leadership is, behaviour that enables and assists others to achieve personal and organizational ambitions and goals. This suggests that leadership might have as much to do with making helpful suggestions as to issuing instructions, as much about listening to other people's ideas as to expounding our own, and as much about gentleness as about toughness. Effectiveness in organizations depends upon leadership emerging appropriately as and when necessary.

We can take the definition further: leadership is helping people to be as effective as (a) they themselves want to be, and (b) they have the potential to be. We need to let go of the inherited belief that leadership is about making people what they are not. Leadership which flows from this more life-enhancing definition has some important features:

● It needs to be seen as a function of a group rather than the role of an individual.
● Leadership can be behaviour which gives power away.
● The aims of leadership should be the increase of self-directedness and the release of energy, imagination and creativity in all those who form the organization.
● Leadership is behaviour which energizes, activates, and increases the capacity of individuals and groups to move ever nearer to shared visions and aims.
● Leadership behaviour is best designed by the followers. Leaders need to seek information from their colleagues about the sort of leadership that suits them best.
● One of the key functions of leadership is to help in the creating of conditions in which people feel motivated to work to the optimum levels of their energy, interest and commitment.

This marks a significant shift in emphasis from traditional definitions of leadership.

> *Box 4.7*
> *Leadership concepts*
> Five particular ideas are central to the development of a more life enhancing concept of leadership:
>
> - Leadership rather than management contains the key to future success.
> - Leadership is a function of all participants in the organization.
> - All of us have a capacity for leadership and exercise it in various parts of our lives.
> - Leadership is dynamic and future oriented, concerned with improvement, development and excellence.
> - Leadership provides a framework within which human potential can more effectively be released.

## Leadership stances

Leadership work involves two distinct but related stances: directional and supportive.

### Directional stance

Leaders need to hold a vision of the organization's purposes, policies and plans. They need to be active in articulating this vision and rallying commitment to it. Leaders are concerned to find ways forward, to generate a clear sense of movement and direction. This may involve identifying new goals, new services and new structures. Leaders have ideas and articulate thoughts that are strong motivators for the working team, creating a directional energy.

Leadership of this sort involves:

- A strong sense of mission for the organization.
- A clear vision of how we want the organization to be.
- A systematic plan for achieving the vision.
- A strong determination to make things work.
- A capacity to share these qualities with colleagues and others.

### Supportive stance

The key resources for any organization are the people who work in it, and leadership is concerned with creating the social and psychological conditions in which they can be enabled to work at their best. This involves:

- deep understanding of others
- sensitivity to to the feelings and needs of others
- trust in their capabilities and intentions
- appreciation of the contributions they make
- constant encouragement.

### Leadership functions

Another perspective involves a consideration of just how many varied roles are involved in leadership and management work in schools. Most will be familiar with the following and could probably add many more.

---

*Box 4.8*
*Leadership functions*
Teachers will be familiar with the following functional activities carried out in connection with their roles.

- philosophers
- parents
- technologists
- communicators
- assessors
- friends
- therapists
- guides
- strategists
- psychologists
- social workers
- teachers
- leaders
- nurses.

---

Leadership involves a staggering variety of tasks, activities and processes. It is fascinating to note how quickly and subtly we can move from one to the other, sometimes carrying out a number of them at the same time.

### Personal resources for leadership

We also need to consider what range of inner resources we possess to carry out our leadership roles effectively and successfully. We have tended to believe that people who occupy leadership positions have, by definition, superior intelligence, skills and qualities than the rest of us. This is by no means the case. What they undoubtedly do have is:

- the belief that they have a leadership contribution to make
- confidence in their capability to make it.

---

Box 4.9
*Personal resources for leadership*
- Constantly developing experience.
- Vision of what we want to achieve.
- Convictions and beliefs about the services we provide.
- Energy to strive and to struggle.
- Sensitivity to the experiences and needs of others.
- Understanding of the challenges involved.
- Capacity to encourage those we interact with.
- Courage to take risks and try things out.
- Presence in the scheme of things.
- Simply being there for others.

---

These are not the qualities usually highlighted in the literature about leadership, but they are very much the ones to the fore in schools and provide a model for other less life-focused organizations.

### Needs-responsive leadership

As well as considering leadership from the leader's own perspective, it is important to have regard for the needs that we have as followers, of our leaders. All of us are needy, and failure to get some very specific needs satisfied, particularly those that contribute to our pattern of motivation, can result in:

- loss of confidence and enthusiasm
- a sense of not being involved and a part of things
- a feeling of being unappreciated and undervalued
- a reduction of job commitment and energy.

These are expensive losses which few organizations can afford. Good leadership is the delicate process of anticipating these needs in others and striving to satisfy them.

Figure 4.5 indicates a range of needs we are likely to experience quite frequently. This provides a useful framework with which to consider and plan our leadership work:

- *Trusting* Conveying to colleagues a belief in their abilities. Resisting the temptation to increase control when things are difficult. Expressing delight at successes and achievements.
- *Listening* Constantly seeking opportunities to listen to current experiences. Asking questions, seeking information, eliciting opinions, delving into details and showing genuine interest and concern.
- *Noticing* Taking note of contributions and providing regular positive feedback on successes and achievements.
- *Encouraging* Empathizing with demands and challenges. Providing support for problem-solving and action-planning.
- *Helping* Offering practical help for those seeking to increase knowledge and develop new skills. Working to create new job and responsibility opportunities

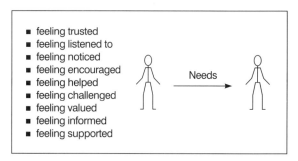

*Figure 4.5* Leadership and individual needs

- *Challenging* Building a climate of systematic and continuous improvement. Constantly helping others to seek new angles, new possibilities and new ideas.
- *Valuing* Providing detailed and specific feedback so that all participants feel a deep sense that their contributions are valued.
- *Informing* Keeping information flowing freely through the organization. Checking that people know.
- *Supporting* Offering practical help as well as moral support. Getting alongside colleagues as often as possible. Providing a helping hand and a listening ear.

### Freedom and authority

One of the key elements in determining how leaders should behave in the pursuit of their aims and aspirations is the relationship between freedom and authority (Rowan, 1992). Freedom is seen as basic human right and we regard those who are in power/coercive relationships to us as having the capacity to inhibit, deny and limit the freedom we crave. If we feel that the way we are treated at work is unreasonably inhibiting our freedom (beyond contractual limits) then there are consequences for both sides. The resulting dynamics create a struggle to protect, defend and fight for more freedom which can in turn tend to stimulate others to repel and limit us. We each take up a position to protect our deep need for freedom and control over our own lives. We can do this by:

- accepting the *status quo* and working within its frameworks
- undermining the *status quo*
- working to transform the *status quo*.

Each of these approaches are at work in most organizations.

One way for leaders to face up to this very basic issue is to see work as a much broader concept than that of providing only the monetary resources to manage our lives. If we accept that work fulfils a number of very important functions in our lives, irrespective of qualifications, status and experience, then we can usefully conceive of the idea of psychological pay-days in addition to financial ones.

---

*Box 4.10*
*Psychological pay-days*
We can be said to have had a psychological pay-day when we:

- feel we are a full partner in the success of the school
- have some degree of self-direction in our work
- are influential in decision-making and school development
- are recognized and valued for the many contributions we make
- experience a sense of achievement
- experience high self-esteem in our role within the school
- are advancing our personal goals in life as well as our professional ones.

---

Given this insight into work it is clearly necessary to go beyond the traditional and conventional notions of leadership with their command and control stances to a way of working with colleagues that taps into their deepest personal and professional needs.

When looked at from the follower's point of view one sees that the satisfaction of individuals needs is a vital function of management work – leadership becomes a way of relating to the colleagues we work with, rather than a requirement to direct and control (Box 4.11).

Achieving mutual understanding is one of the most demanding challenges of leadership work, living as we do in a world where the potential for misunderstanding is so enormous. Graham Webb (1996) observes: 'Learning that true understanding is rarely developed through spiteful dismissal or crushed argument is a long and painful process.' He also quotes Palmer (in Webb, 1996) as saying: 'The keys to understanding are not manipulation and control but participation and openness, not knowledge but experience, not methodology but dialectic.'

---

*Box 4.11*
*Leadership: essential elements*
In his study of supportive relationships David Howe (1993) has found that we look for three essential elements in a supportive relationship:

*Acceptance*
the creation of a secure emotional base for the relationship, in which we feel accepted by the leader as a person worthy of respect.

*Understanding*
feeling that the leader appreciates the many complex factors that lead us to behave as we do.

*Dialogue*
the need to use communication to reach understandings and acquire meanings.

---

For the leader this requires an understanding that a person's power and potential to work effectively lie inside them, not with the leader. What the leader must do is strive to build a powerful accepting and understanding relationship with colleagues and use dialogue to help bring that inner potential to life in specific and particular ways in the interests of the school. This suggest that leaders need to work more through influence and impact than through a formal reliance on power and control (Figure 4.6).

What we want in our leadership work is to have an influence and impact on our colleagues. We want to behave in ways that make a difference to the ways people think about and discharge their responsibilities. The capacity to be influential depends upon our own capabilities and the basic values we hold about the nature of leadership. John Nicholson (1992) has suggested there are five key principles:

- being prepared
- being focused
- being flexible

- being convinced
- being convincing.

These factors certainly help in preparing for a piece of proactive leadership, but we also need to consider the communication factors in relation to the individual concerned, and to be in touch with those

| Leadership by influence and impact | Leadership by power and control |
| --- | --- |
| Gives autonomy to individuals and groups | Makes decisions alone |
| Frees people to 'do their thing' | Gives orders |
| Expresses own ideas and feelings | Directs subordinates' behaviour |
| Stimulates independence in thought and action | Exercises authority over people |
| Delegates and gives full authority | Coerces where necessary |
| Seeks and offers feedback | Instructs and advises |
| Encourages reliance on self-evaluation | Evaluates others |
| Finds rewards in the development and achievements of others | Gives rewards |

*Figure 4.6* Contrasting leadership styles

factors which will determine whether or not the five factors above will be successful. In other words, leadership is conducted through encounters in which there are two main concerns:

- to achieve professional goals
- to communicate effectively.

The most effective leaders are the ones who are able to create the most appropriate balance between directional factors and supportive ones. If we are to be really effective in our leadership work, our colleagues need to experience the basis of power and control as residing within themselves, and not as something that we as leaders can confer.

One of the crucial elements frequently referred to in the analysis of organizations is the presence or absence of trust, and it is central to the debate about power in relation to leadership. Handy (1976) illustrates the trust/control relationship by suggesting that the sum of trust plus

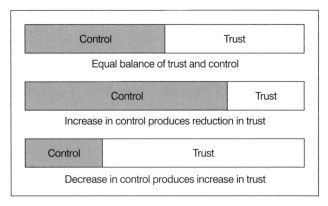

*Figure 4.7* Trust and control

control is always constant (Figure 4.7). Handy further observes that giving trust is not easy because:

- It requires having confidence in the subordinate to do the job.
- Like a leap in the dark trust must be given if it is to be received.
- Trust is a fragile commodity, like glass, once it is shattered it is never the same again.
- Trust must be reciprocal. It is no good the superior trusting the subordinates if their trust is not returned.

But trust can be created if:

- Participants are involved in the selection of key colleagues and have some say in leader appointments (sometimes found in task cultures, seldom in role cultures).
- The territory of trust is clearly defined for each individual and is not violated.
- There is control of ends, not means.

It is through the countless interpersonal transactions of the school day that peoples lives are changed, organizational improvements are made, dreams are realized and needs are met. We need more understanding of the complex psychological dynamics of those snatched moments in corridors. While we cannot plan for these unexpected incidents, we can be prepared for them, appreciating that they present golden opportunities to encourage and support. It is not so much a matter of what is said in these moments, as with what our basic stance in these transactions is like. David Howe (1993) suggests that three ingredients need to be present if the relationship is to work effectively:

- *Acceptance* The creation of a secure emotional base to the transaction.

- *Understanding*  An appreciation and sensitivity to the felt experience of the other person.
- *Dialogue*  The communication of meaning and understanding.

These contrast vividly with the leadership toxins that Senge (1990) describes. He suggests that leaders are at their most ineffective when:

- they try too hard to get people committed
- they set the direction for others
- they alone make the key decisions
- they sustain a traditional view of leadership based on assumptions of people's powerlessness, their lack of personal vision and the presence of faults which have to be remedied.

Life-focused leadership is essentially a catalytic process, helping others to bring about changes in themselves. Catalytic energy is supplied to the other person who has the potential for effective action, but that potentiality is not yet activated. Through dialogue with the leader, that potential energy is activated and transformed into kinetic energy. This catalytic capacity is created when a complex combination of attitudes, stances and interpersonal skills crystallize within the transaction.

Howe (1993) emphasizes the importance of the stances we take in these situations and highlights three:

- *Attentiveness*  Offering undivided attention in a warm and caring way, and showing a real interest in the other's concerns.

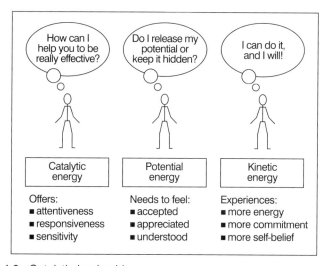

*Figure 4.8*  Catalytic leadership

- *Responsiveness* Verbal and non-verbal responding which conveys understanding and which helps the other person to solve their own problems and make their own decisions.
- *Sensitivity* Demonstrating a caring acceptance of the other person's feelings in the situation.

Figure 4.8 attempts to capture some of the elements of this complex process.

Above all the factors discussed in this chapter, leadership is essentially a process of constant learning. The complex phenomena of any organization, and particularly of schools, will always be too much for complete understanding. These phenomena are in a constant state of change, affected by the endless incidents and events that characterize school life. Leaders must never cease in their curiosity, in their determination to learn and to understand. The success of their interventions will very much depend on how well they attend to this learning.

---

- Reflect on the definitions of leadership discussed at the beginning of this section. How do you define it? What for you are its essential components?
- In what ways is leadership work in schools similar to, and different from, leadership in other types of organization?
- How would you define your own personal resources for leadership (Box 4.9)?
- Consider the factors identified in Figure 4.5 in terms of your own pattern of needs, and in terms of your leadership work with others.
- When do you consider you have had a psychological pay-day (Box 4.10)?
- Consider the dynamics of the factors outlined in Figure 4.8. How do these relate to your own leadership style?

# 5 Reviewing progress

In business we are always passing from one significant moment to another significant moment, and the leader's task is pre-eminently to understand *the moment of passing*. This is why the leader's task is so difficult, why it requires great qualities – the most delicate and sensitive perceptions, imagination and insight, and at the same time courage and faith.
(Follett)

## Introduction

A great deal of attention has been given to the processes of evaluation and assessment in recent years. This has been useful in countering a tendency to regard evaluation as an afterthought, something we do at the end. Review is a vital element in strategic management and needs to be handled with the same care we give to planning and operating. But it also needs to be seen in a wider context than the current preoccupation with measured scores and league tables. Evaluation is about understanding, without which we can never manage effectively.

This chapter will:

- consider the factors which make review and evaluation in schools so challenging
- note the distinction between implicit and explicit evaluation
- place review and evaluation within the whole strategic process
- examine the essential elements of review management and consider a range of review frameworks
- explore the issue of quality in the review process
- discuss the theory of praxis and its application in schools.

## Review and evaluation

In strategic terms, review and evaluation constitutes the final link in the 4P development chain and the third phase of the model introduced in Chapter 2 (Figure 5.1). Schools, like all other organizations, need to carry out reviews and evaluations in order to discover the extent to which plans are brought successfully to fruition.

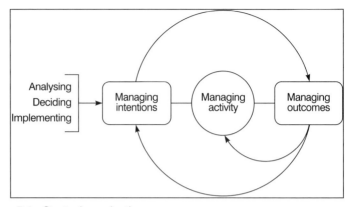

*Figure 5.1* Strategic evaluation

---

*Box 5.1*
*Review and evaluation*
A variety of purposes are served when review and evaluation is carried out:

- monitoring policies and practices
- acquiring data and information
- measuring success and achievement
- gaining insights and understandings
- identifying problems and difficulties
- making professional judgements
- exercising accountability
- providing feedback
- learning about the school
- identifying areas for change and development.

---

In schools, the processes involved in review and evaluation are both intricate and varied. A number of factors, specifically relating to the schooling process, need to be considered.

## Complexity

Learning is a process of continuous growth and development, requiring almost continuous feedback for it to operate effectively. Evaluation is an integral part of this process, both for the pupils in the management of their learning, and for the teachers in planning and managing appropriate experiences. In few other organizations are the products of the enterprise required to have a view about their own development.

The variety and range of the elements involved in learning make its accurate evaluation very complex indeed, and recent attempts to devise simple procedures can only succeed in producing somewhat superficial and incomplete data.

## Invisibility

The learning process is largely invisible – it takes place within us, making it difficult to observe, and therefore to assess. It requires a painstaking and continuous process of enquiry, observation and transaction to understand its complex workings.

## Individuality

Styles of learning, rates of development and patterns of learning capability are configured in different ways for each individual pupil. The decisions teachers make with their pupils about the course and management of their learning have to take account of different formulations of thinking, motivation, previous experience, particular mood at the time and a range of other personal, social and psychological factors as well.

In reviewing the work of teachers we are faced with similar challenges. Teachers, like their pupils, are different from each other, and it is not easy to separate the purely professional factors in their work from the more personal ones such as warmth, approachability and empathy – each of which is likely to affect significantly the ways in which pupils learn.

## Integral

In schools, review is much more of an integral process than it is in many other types of organization and this makes it difficult to separate from the planning and operating phases of strategy. In many business organizations, review tends to be carried out by a specialist department, often called Quality Control. Those who work in such departments spend virtually all of their time in the measurement and assessment of company products and processes.

The strategic work involved in teaching is embedded – the planning, operating and evaluating elements are more dynamically enmeshed with each other and are never static. Learning does not cease at the end of the school day, the process is always in perpetual motion and always changing. Even the apparently small decisions a teacher makes about a pupil's learning will involve some combination of the three strategic phases.

In schools we are attempting to measure and assess the complexities of a largely organic and haphazard process, in which countless variables interact with each other, often in unpredictable and indeterminate ways.

### Multi-layered

In schools, the review and evaluation process has two levels:

- the evaluation of the learning taking place within each individual pupil
- the evaluation of the school and how it manages that learning.

It is important to make a distinction between the evaluation of learning and the evaluation of performance. The first is concerned with the dynamic and continuous process of growth and development, the second with the measured application of learning against established norms or standards. The first helps us to manage the learning process, the second enables us to grade.

### Human experience

Schooling is concerned with a human process. Learning is an experience of great complexity, difficult to understand and demanding to assess. Schools are concerned with changes in their pupils, almost on a minute to minute basis. Methods of review and evaluation that can be applied to simpler products, particularly manufactured ones, are not a sensible option for a school. One of the dangers of wanting rigid objectivity in school assessment is that we end up measuring only the easily measurable. The temptation to apply mechanical methods to a human process is understandable, particularly in a climate of rivalry and competition. But schooling is not a competition, it is a process of the utmost delicacy in which the learning potential of each pupil has to be nourished, guided and supported. Becoming a statistic does not help a pupil to learn.

### Professional judgement

Most of the important questions involved in the evaluation of learning require high levels of professional judgement. Yet it is this aspect of our work – the making of professional judgements about learning and teaching – which is currently so distrusted by politicians. What we have seen in recent years have been attempts to create simple ways of assessing pupil performance through procedures which reduce reliance on professional judgement. The difficulty then is that we obtain data that is almost meaningless outside its context. Paradoxically we have seen an OFSTED framework developed which relies almost totally on judgement – the formulation of opinions about school performance by delegated observers over a short period of time.

In the years ahead we will need to move beyond this obsession with the instrumental and mechanistic and accept that the assessment of learning is inordinately complex, requiring the most painstaking and profound insights we can bring to it. If our evaluation is crude, then the whole process is likely to become so too.

> - Jot down those aspects of your role which have a specifically review aspect to them (Box 5.1).
> - Consider your views of assessment in schools in relation to the factors outlined in this section.
> - What is your experience of the OFSTED procedure?

## Implicit and explicit evaluation

It is important to understand the distinction between implicit and explicit evaluation.

### Implicit evaluation

This is where we engage in the review process in order to be able to take the decisions to move classroom activity forward. It is activated on countless occasions in each lesson, and concerns the individual's relationship to a learning task or activity.

It is also used in the management aspects of school life, enabling individual managers to make adjustments to systems and to keep the strategic work of the school operating effectively.

### Explicit evaluation

This is where we operate deliberately in review mode to discover a specific range of data and information about the work of the school. This type of review tends to be concerned with such questions as:

- Is the quality of learning improving?
- Are pupils' achievements commensurate with their aptitude?
- What difficulties are particular pupils experiencing?
- Which teaching methods are working best?
- How well is the timetable operating?
- Is subject leadership effective?

Obtaining satisfactory answers to such questions as these is extremely difficult and there are no simple evaluation methods which will provide us with the categoric answers we are under so much pressure to provide.

## The strategic dimension

In strategic terms, review and evaluation is a dynamic process which provides the information required to guide the school on its journey towards its goals and visions.

> *Box 5.2*
> *Narrow and broad strategy*
> It is useful to distinguish between two approaches to review and evaluation:
>
> *Narrow strategy*
> Assessing the academic performance of pupils in order to publish results.
>
> *Broad strategy*
> Learning about how the school works in order to develop and improve.
>
> It is with this broader type of approach that management and leadership work in schools is involved.

The relationship of the review process to the other aspects of the strategic model is illustrated in Figure 5.2.

The review exercises indicated by the backward/upward-flowing arrows, suggest a systematic comparing of outcomes with intentions. The strategy can be applied to large-scale exercises like the school development plan, as well as to smaller-scale activities within specific curriculum areas or pupils' own learning programmes. It involves using the documented descriptions of the end results specified for a particular development, and relating these to the outcomes that have been produced. This will establish one of three possible positions:

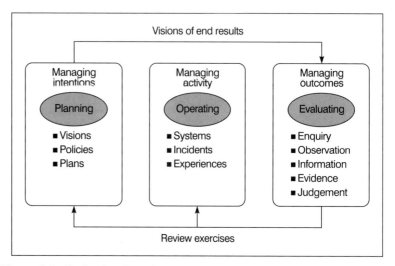

*Figure 5.2* Evaluation: broad strategy

1 Outcomes are commensurate with intentions.
2 Outcomes exceed intentions.
3 Outcomes fall short of intentions.

If outcomes are largely as planned, this indicates successful planning and implementation. The school will want to consider whether some raising of aims and expectations will bring even greater success, or whether the costs of producing such outcomes have been dispropor-tionate to the resources available and cannot be sustained in the future.

If the outcomes have exceeded the intentions then it will be important to establish why this was so. Perhaps intentions were too modest, in which case the planning may need to be reviewed. Perhaps the methodologies used have been more effective than expected, in which case these will need to be examined to identify the precise causes of success so that they can be more widely adopted.

Similarly, if outcomes fall short of intentions, then it will be necessary to consider whether planning was too ambitious, or if problems arose in the implementation and operational stage.

## Sightlines

The process of review and evaluation is not confined to looking back, it involves using the information and insights we acquire to look to the

---

*Box 5.3*
*Multiple sightlines*
Review consciousness is a vital quality of an effective manager. It involves the capacity to see the school with a variety of perspectives that deepen understanding and illuminate complex-ity. Among the different sightlines to cultivate are:

- insights
- foresights
- aftersights
- throughsights
- oversights
- undersights
- sidesights
- outsights
- frontsights
- backsights.

Each of these sets the review process with a different perspective, each of which has the potential to produce valuable ideas and information about the school and its complex processes.

future. One of the benefits of an implicit process is that we do not make a formal separation between plans and outcomes. We see them as essential and related parts of the same strategic system.

One of the qualities we need to develop in our leadership and management work is a capacity to work through a variety of perspectives.

Perspectives consciousness is a vital quality for managers to have. The cultivating of views other than our own of how an operation works, helps us to see the broad picture more completely, providing us with the information and understanding we need to work effectively with our colleagues.

---

- Reflect on the review processes at work in your school. How do they operate?
- In what ways does the distinction between implicit and explicit evaluation manifest itself in your experience?
- Consider the concept of multiple sightlines (Box 5.3). Use each of the sightlines to help you gain a more comprehensive understanding of your school at work.

---

## Managing review and evaluation

In defining the processes involved in evaluation we need to bear in mind the difference in operational practice between the implicit and explicit aspects referred to earlier.

---

*Box 5.4*
*Event or process?*

*Event evaluation (explicit)*
Conducting evaluation as a set of precise, scheduled exercises, often managed with objectivity in mind.

*Process evaluation (implicit)*
Using evaluation as part of an integrative strategic process which is taking place all the time. It values both subjective and objective data in the constant search for insight and understanding.

---

Figure 5.2 suggests that there are five essential management issues involved in the management of outcomes (Whitaker, 1997):

- enquiry
- observation

- information
- evidence
- judgement.

Let us examine each of these elements in turn.

## *Enquiry*

The most powerful driving force behind the review process is knowing clearly what it is that we want to discover. A useful starting point is to pose a question. For example:

- How many pupils in Year 6 have attained Level 4 in science?
- How effective is our information technology teaching?

The first is a closed question requiring only a piece of attainment testing. The information required is clear and can be provided as a statistic. Many enquiries about pupils and their learning can be posed in this focused and closed way. The second is more open-ended and ambiguous. We are not clear exactly what we are asking. In order to clarify the nature of our enquiry we need to ask more specific questions. For example:

- What methods and techniques constitute our approach to information technology teaching?
- On what principles are these based?
- What are our current visions and intentions for information technology in the school?
- To what extent are our pupils' achievements commensurate with their aptitude and potential for information technology?

These more focused questions help to clarify the various aspects of a possible enquiry, but they still raise significant further questions:

- What constitutes a teaching method or technique?
- On what basis are teaching methods determined in this school?
- What specific intentions and targets have we currently set for ourselves in information technology?
- What do we mean by aptitude and potential for learning in information technology?

This emphasizes just how complex are the processes of school management, and just what intricate and philosophical issues are involved. The literature of the teaching profession has left many of these questions and issues unattended to, and as a profession we rely less than virtually all others on documented and agreed method-ologies. Unlike surgeons whose practice is based on defined procedures, or architects who draw on established formulae for such things as load-bearing walls, teachers have worked with a series of rather vague rules of thumb. Perhaps this reflects the enormous difficulty of trying to define pedagogy and teaching methodology in an area populated with so many complex variables.

It helps to recall the 4P development chain in the context of setting up a review enquiry:

- *Purpose* 'We want to conduct a review in order to . . .'
- *Policy* 'Our review policy states . . .'
- *Practice* 'What we will need to do in order to conduct the review is . . .'
- *Product* 'What we will end up with when the review is completed is . . .'

It can also help to avoid questions altogether and instead formulate the enquiry as a task brief:

- List the pupils who have achieved Level 4 in science in Year 6.
- Carry out a review of current information technology work in the school.

It is when review enquiries involve considerations of practice as well as the products of learning work that the challenges of review management are compounded. The second enquiry above has more of the characteristics of detective work about it than the somewhat straightforward assessment of science attainments. Yet it is the second review that will contain the most valuable insights into how to manage school development and improvement and to be able to identify new visions and intentions.

## Observation

Observation is often regarded as a deliberate and discrete activity that takes place intermittently in schools. It evokes images of clipboards, observation schedules and trying to be separate from what we are attempting to observe. This sort of observation can be a very useful exercise when particular information is required, but it is by no means the only approach. It is through the implicit process of observing what is happening as we conduct the day-to-day business of the school, that we gain the vast majority of information about how things are going. We do not require trained observers to tell us whether it is a wet playtime or whether a child is on task. We know these things through our constant attention to, and awareness of, what is happening. It is too easy to dismiss this awareness as entirely subjective, but then most of what happens in learning is subjective. We need to appreciate that it is through our conscious and continuous awareness that we acquire the information we need to manage our affairs.

---

*Box 5.5*
*Skilled noticing*
Skilled noticing involves using our observational skills as we go about our classroom or management work in a directed and precise way, searching for information that can tell us about progress and development.

We need to develop the habit of capturing significant incidents and behaviour, making sure that we record it as evidence which we can use later to help us form judgements about achievements and outcomes.

If we have done our planning work well, we will have specified, often in some detail, the exact nature of the outcomes we are working towards, and we can be alert to signs that they are being achieved.

---

## Information

While the formal processes of school evaluation will rely on the acquisition of *hard* data – performance figures, test results and pupil assessments – it is vital to appreciate there is a whole world of *soft* data that is vital if a full understanding of school effectiveness is to be achieved. Evaluation must not only focus on the results themselves, it must also give attention to the means. The exposition of data only tells us what has happened, and exposition without explanation is of little value to a school which will want to know how to build on successes, and how to remedy shortfalls and inadequacies. Producing the exposition – the hard data – is comparatively straightforward. Acquiring explanation is more difficult, involving enquiry into the complexities of how things happen, who did what, how others reacted, what problems were identified and what solutions were considered.

---

*Box 5.6*
*Soft data*
A great deal of management relies on *soft* data to provide insights and explanations:

- thoughts and feelings
- hopes and fears
- worries and concerns
- rumours
- hearsay
- gossip
- body language
- casual conversation
- speculation
- the grapevine.

---

We learn most about how we are doing and what is happening by reading expressions on colleagues' faces, noticing their gestures and picking up their voice tones. This soft data relates especially to the unpredictable encounters we all experience every day at school, and contributes to a steadily accumulating bank of information and ideas about how the school works, what people are thinking about, how they are feeling and levels of job satisfaction and stress.

### Evidence

We need evidence to judge effectiveness. Just as in courts of law, this evidence needs to be specific, detailed and factual. Impressions and opinions are not sufficient grounds to assure us that the conclusions we draw about the quality of our work are safe and secure. The systematic gathering of evidence involves four particular sources:

- observation: what we see and hear
- enquiry: through dialogue with learners and others
- material: pupils' work, documents, records
- measurements: results of assessments, sampling and testing.

### Judgement

It is not until appropriate data is assembled that evaluation can take place. This part of the process requires judgements to be made in relation to the intentions originally specified. The key question that drives all evaluation is – have we achieved our declared intentions? We can only answer this when we have made a rigorous comparison between the specified aims and the manifest outcomes. The accuracy of the judgements will not only depend upon the range and quality of the evidence assembled, but also on the thoroughness of the observational work we engage in and record.

Well-managed evaluation is vital to enable us to identify our strengths and difficulties, to know where to plan new initiatives, where to provide more support and where to spread the techniques of effective practice.

---

- Consider the challenges involved in defining review enquiries. Try drafting some very precise review enquiry tasks related to your own evaluation role.
- List some of the challenges involved in the process of observation in schools – both of children's learning and of teachers' work in classrooms.
- What constitutes *hard* data for you? How much importance do you attach to *soft* data?
- Reflect on the ways that you gather evidence in your role and how you make judgements about quality and effectiveness.

# Review frameworks

## *Systems theory*

In the management of review and evaluation work it is important to appreciate the significance of the organizational setting within which school activity takes place. The intricacies of human behaviour and a constantly changing pattern of encounters and relationships make the process of analysis and understanding within schools very challenging indeed. We need to be aware of the dangers of making judgements on insubstantial information and evidence, recognizing that there may be far more factors and variables affecting an issue than we believed, or are capable of discerning.

Evaluation work is more difficult in human systems than in mechanical ones, and it is because of this that some insight into general systems theory can help.

---

*Box 5.7*
*Systems theory*
A system can be defined as an integrated whole whose essential properties arise from the relationships between its parts. In schools these variables consist of all those involved in school life. Each of these participants, too, are complex clusters of dynamic and constantly changing variables, difficult to pin down and describe accurately. Daily life in a school is an intricate and continuously changing system which defies easy explanation of definition.

---

Human behaviour is an untidy business, where there are significant differences between what we observe people doing and what they themselves may be thinking and feeling inside. *Systems thinking* is the process of striving to understand particular phenomena within the context of the larger whole. In other words the incidents and events experienced by pupils in science and information technology are not happenings isolated from the wider context. The experiences in a Year 6 science lesson in a primary school may have a relationship to a pupil's capacity to learn successfully in information technology later in the secondary school. Many of the relationships between the small variables are tenuous and difficult to observe and isolate, but we must always appreciate that they are there.

Systems cannot be understood simply by analysis. The properties of the parts are not discrete and intrinsic, they can only be understood in the context of the larger whole. Three particular aspects of a complex system are particularly useful to understand – pattern, structure and process (Capra, 1996).

*Pattern*

This is the configuration of relationships among the different components of the system, and these determine their essential characteristics. In other words, how well a pupil learns will to some extent depend upon the pattern of relationships that are present in a classroom between the pupils themselves, between individual pupils and the teacher and between the teacher and the class as a whole.

*Structure*

This is the physical embodiment of the pattern of organization and will include, for example, the curriculum and how it is organized, the rules and regulations governing behaviour, the roles and responsibilities of staff and the allocation of pupils to different teaching groups.

*Process*

This refers to the dynamic activity involved in the system and how the variables interact with each other. It will include, for example, interpersonal encounters, teaching activity, how people react to incidents and events and how individuals strive to satisfy their needs.

It is important to keep emphasizing that schools are complex systems which defy simplistic analysis. Therefore the management of review and evaluation, particularly in relation to the more open-ended enquiries we will want to pursue is fraught with challenges. This does not mean that we should avoid it, but rather that we appreciate the dangers of being certain and categoric in our judgements. We may get near to the truth of why things happen as they do in schools, but we must always allow for the fact that our understanding is never likely to be complete. The scientist Werner Heisenberg (1962) has asserted: 'What we observe is not nature itself, but nature exposed to our method of questioning.'

This systems framework can help us to make our method of questioning more reflective of the complexity present within the school system.

**Accountability**

Issues of accountability are never far from our minds these days and it is vital to be clear about our responsibilities to share information and explanations with those who are concerned with the school.

The management of review and evaluation involves a wide community of interests. We can distinguish between internal interests, the pupils and teachers within the school, and external interests, parents, governors, local authorities and central government. The authority to evaluate exists both within the system through regulation, and within the professional roles of staff through tradition. This raises the issues of autonomy and freedom referred to in Chapter 4. A further accountability issue concerns the question of who evaluation is undertaken for. Do we evaluate in order to prove to those in authority that we are discharging our responsibilities as intended, or to enable the internal participants to receive information that will enable progress to be made? The answer is far from simple. Both aspects of accountability are necessary and important, but each has different purposes and, therefore, different methodologies. While a set of examination results may provide those in external authority with the information they require, bald scores in an examination do not enable individual pupils to know how to increase the quality of their learning.

This brings us back to the tricky issue discussed in Chapter 2 about whether pupils are workers, clients or products. In their roles as workers and products, then, the pupils themselves will need to be the objects of evaluation. In their roles as clients they will need to be the agents of review enquiries into the services they partake of. The question of whether pupils should evaluate the experiences they are offered at school has been largely and conveniently ignored. That pupils do evaluate is not in dispute, the question is whether in the future we can afford to ignore the data they possess and risk losing a vital source of information and insight into how the school is working.

We also need to give a new emphasis to self-managed evaluation. Pupils, like their teachers, are skilled noticers of what goes on around them and they are very capable of making perceptive judgements about their own learning. Although they are inevitably involved in self-assessment, this is not regarded as appropriate, relevant or important. It is sad that the OFSTED framework provides no significant place for the gathering of data from pupils themselves.

It is the learners themselves who have the greatest interest in learning. We need to help them to build skills in assessment and evaluation in order that they can operate the strategic approach for themselves. Developing pupil skills in evaluation will facilitate the journey from dependence to interdependence, encouraging a more formative sense of self-responsibility than is presently encouraged in the schooling system. Self-evaluation is a vital component in the process of becoming, of systematically unfolding our potentialities in the world.

## Appraisal

Appraisal is now part of the professional environment. The introduction of appraisal into the education service has been greeted with some suspicion because it has been seen as a system of judging the worth of an individual teacher's performance. This is very unfortunate and unnecessary, because appraisal has the potential to be a highly powerful aid to personal and professional development. It is also important to realize that appraisal is something we have always done. We are forever appraising situations, working out costs and benefits, estimating risk and identifying more effective ways forward. For most of us, appraisal has served as a largely unstructured reflection on our experience, and an important means of learning from and through those experiences.

If a structured process of appraisal is an aid to professional development and the learning of teachers, it is important to ask how it can be utilized in the service of learner development. It is just as important for pupils to submit to systematic review aspects of their learning as it is for their teachers.

### Review meetings

A review meeting provides an opportunity for those involved in managing a development project of task to come together to take stock of progress to date. Two distinct types of review meetings are necessary: task review and process review.

#### Task review

A task review enables us to compare outcomes with intentions and to measure the effectiveness of a project. It is here that the well-structured goal statements produced at the planning stage are so useful. These can now be used as checking devices to assess progress and achievement. While a major review meeting will be necessary at the end of any project, interim task reviews are also vital if difficulties are to be dealt with and adjustments and fine tuning to the project's action plan made.

Of equal importance is the opportunity to consider the processes involved in the management of any project. This we can refer to as the process review:

#### Process review

Process reviews are concerned with the conduct and management of a project or task, and focus on how the different aspects of the project are being managed, how effective the leadership is, how team relationships are working and how particular methods and techniques are being used.

A useful way to conduct a process review meeting is to produce forms designed to encourage reflective thinking about the process (Figure 5.3). Participants in a process review meeting can jot down their own perceptions, observations and experiences. These can then be shared and the emerging issues explored.

| What we did that was successful | What we can do to repeat this success in the future |
|---|---|
| What we did that created difficulties | What we can do to overcome these difficulties in the future |
| Specific contributions that were especially helpful | Individual skills we need to develop |

*Figure 5.3* Process review form

---

*Box 5.8*

*Review meetings*

Review meetings should form an integral and regular part of the management of any development project.

A useful procedure is to distribute copies of the review forms and allow a few minutes reflection time in which to make notes on the forms, take each category in turn. Then go round the table inviting each person to share their reflections.

Once all personal points have been declared and noted, preferably on a flipchart or whiteboard where everyone can see them, general discussion can follow in which the review team strives for insights and understandings.

Process reviews are vital in enabling us to:

- share feelings about the project and its management
- highlight successes and difficulties
- identify areas for project development
- provide feedback to individual team members
- make plans for future teamwork
- appreciate the process of working together
- identify areas for individual development
- build confidence and team spirit
- develop the organizational culture
- help the school work towards its vision.

Review should never be an afterthought, it should be seen as a vital part of the dynamic strategic process. Review purposes and procedures should be established at the planning stage of any project and allowed an appropriate share of resources and funding, particularly an allocation of time in which to conduct it.

> ● Use Capra's three categories – pattern, structure and process – to review those areas of school life for which you are responsible.
> ● How do you manage the accountability required in your role?
> ● How important do you think it is to be clear about the distinction between task review and process review?

## Perspectives on quality

In recent years there has been much discussion and activity around issues of quality. Some organizations have vigorously embraced this management concept and introduced a total quality management approach. Often this constitutes what has become known as a *quality assurance* approach to management.

> *Box 5.9*
> *Quality assurance*
> (Murgatroyd and Morgan, 1993)
> Quality assurance refers to the determination of standards, appropriate methods and quality requirements by an expert body, accompanied by a process of inspection or evaluation that examines the extent to which practice meets these standards.

The OFSTED project is clearly an example of quality assurance in the educational world. But for those involved in the internal management of schools, quality does not have to be only of this hard edged, accountability kind, it can be used as a more empowering concept, providing valuable insights into the ways schools operate and the successes they can achieve.

One way to define quality is to say that it exists as a relationship between expectation and outcome. When a product or service falls below our expectation we are often disappointed and frustrated, and sometimes angry when the supplier does little to remedy our dissatisfaction. We regard this as low quality. On the other hand when a product or service exceeds our expectations then we are pleased and consider it to be of high quality. Central to the concept of quality in organizations is the idea that a product or service needs to go beyond mere satisfaction and achieve delight – a deep sense of enjoyment with what we have received. This concept helps us to appreciate that review and evaluation activities are concerned with our experience as well as our behaviour, particularly with the feelings and emotions that are aroused when a product or service is received. Measurements and standards rarely produce sufficient insight, and in the consideration of quality there tends to be a more significant subjective element present, based more on felt experience than rational thought. It is this aspect of quality which can be so useful in schools.

Learning is essentially a personal experience. It is not something that is done to us but something that we do for ourselves. Our capacities to learn effectively are certainly affected by those who bear responsibility with us for fostering our childhood growth and development – parents and teachers. But we should appreciate too, that in the management of learning in schools, we need to hold both objective and subjective elements in a dynamic balance.

The concept of quality offers a significant breakthrough in our thinking. It can be considered as a synthesizing quality bringing the tensions between objective reality and subjective reality into a powerful alliance. Figure 5.4 illustrates this.

John Nye (unpublished article) has observed that it was quality that Roberts Pirsig's character was pursuing in *Zen and the Art of Motorcycle Maintenance* (Pirsig, 1978):

> But the biggest clue seemed to be their expressions. They were hard to explain. Good natured, friendly, easy going – and uninvolved. They were like spectators. You had the feeling that they had just wandered

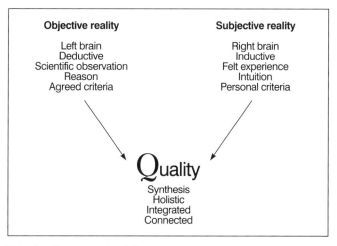

*Figure 5.4* Quality: a synthesizing concept

in there themselves and someone had handed them a wrench. There was no identification with the job. No saying 'I am a mechanic.' At 5pm or whenever their eight hours were in, you knew they would cut it off and not have another thought about their job. They were already trying not to have any thoughts about their job.

So quality is not only confined to the product or service itself, it applies especially to our experience of it. The mechanics in Pirsig's book had separated objective reality – their work, from subjective reality – their lives, and were unable to create a powerful connection between the two. So it is with many of our pupils in schools, and some of their teachers too.

It is the reality balance which is so important in schools. It is not enough for pupils to achieve high standards, it is vital to the quality of their learning that they find their work in school a deeply rich and satisfying experience. In providing effective leadership for our schools we need to rise above the conflict between objective visions of education and subjective ones if we are to help schools to rise above their increasingly utilitarian tendency. Schooling is as much about quality of living as it is about academic achievement.

As we engage in the management process and seek to understand how our schools work, we can be helped by further quality concepts. These are outlined in Figure 5.5.

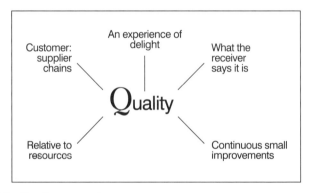

*Figure 5.5*  Quality concepts

### Delight

We need to strive for delight as an experience of all school members. Aiming to create conditions where both pupils and staff experience their work as challenging, interesting and deeply satisfying must be one of the key aims of anyone with management responsibility. The evaluation process needs to give attention to the felt experience of pupils and staff, enquiring into the causes of frustration and disappointment as well as to those of pleasure and delight.

## Client experience

Quality is what the client says it is, not what the organization claims it to be. This principle of quality thinking helps us to place experience right at the heart of the management process, and to promote an approach to education which is life focused. The directional tendency discussed in Chapter 3 is one of the key ingredients in managing, and attention to how pupils and staff experience their time in school is a crucial factor in creating quality and determining success and achievement.

## Small improvements

The pace of change requires an appreciation that development is nowadays achieved through continuous increments, rather than through grand gestures and major innovations. Quality management is built on the idea that:

- anything can be made a little better
- there is no such thing as an insignificant improvement
- no part of school life is too small for concern or attention.

## Relative to resources

As well as relationships between expectations and outcomes, quality can also exist as a relationship between intention and resources. Quality cannot be conceived in absolute terms – a Rolls-Royce Silver Shadow is of better quality than a Ford Fiesta. It is important to consider providing value relative to the resources available. This means not only value for money, but value for time available, value for aptitude available and value for energy available. We need to release ourselves from the hook of absolute perfection. This is usually far too expensive these days, and only results in frustration and stress brought on through guilt, a sense of inadequacy and a belief that we are just not up to it. Instead, we need to think in terms of a *good enough job*. This means that expectations may need to be modified. Perhaps our schools are, after all, doing a good enough job given present circumstances and the level of resources currently available to them. It could be argued that we should be delighted with the performance of our schools, given such disapproval, low funding and overdemand.

## Customer: supplier chains

These are another of the central ideas behind quality management thinking. Murgatroyd and Morgan (1993) observe that schools involve a chain of relationships between what we might call customers and suppliers: 'Teachers are the suppliers of services to pupils and parents;

secretaries are suppliers of services to teachers; school administrators are suppliers of services to teachers; teachers supply services to each other. There are internal customers (those who work for the school). There are also external customers (those who demand services from the school).' This complex chain of relationships gives rise to all the work that schools are concerned with. Murgatroyd and Morgan further state:

> If these processes and chains are managed well, with a constant focus on high performance and improvement, then quality achievements follow. What is important is that attention is given to the managing of *processes*, because processes produce outcomes. Far too much attention has been focused on securing outcomes, no matter what the process looks like – yet it is process quality and effectiveness that leads to *sustainable* quality outcomes.

The concept of quality is particularly useful in education, focusing as it does on an appropriate balance between objective and subjective elements, as well as to the vital synthesizing factors identified in Figure 5.4.

---

- Compare the essence of two recent experiences – one that you felt to be of high quality, and the other of low quality.
- Consider the quotation from *Zen and the Art of Motorcycle Maintenance*. How does the observation relate to your experience of schools?
- Take each of the quality concepts (Figure 5.4) in turn and consider them in relation to your management work.

---

## Praxis

Praxis is a concept used by the Brazilian educator Paulo Freire (1976) to describe the process of action and reflection in the management of human affairs. He suggests that when we reflect on our actions and direct the learning gained from this to future actions, we have more power to transform the structures and patterns that need changing in our lives. The concept is a useful one in helping us to determine the means by which we can seek to understand the complexities of school life and work to change and develop them. In his writings Freire establishes a number of key concepts:

- *Culture of silence* A lack of awareness we sometimes experience of the forces at work in school life which combine together to determine outcomes. If we maintain silence about our deep inner

thoughts and concerns we engage in a conspiracy of silence and prevent the organization from developing the necessary under-standings from which change and development can spring.
- *Raising awareness* The process through which we expose our hunches, concerns, ideas and misgivings to examination, thereby deepening awareness of important organizational realities affecting our work in school.
- *Dialogue* Talking with others in a climate of open enquiry about the issues and concerns affecting the school, thereby sharing perceptions and experiences and determining possible lines of development.

Freire believed that all people have the potential to become more than they currently are, and that by engaging in the process of action – reflection – action they will be more able to work with others to understand and improve their current situations.

Through praxis we create a dynamic relationship between what we do and how we think and feel about what we have done. This reflexive process enables us both to derive insights and understandings about previous actions, and to take account of them in future actions. It is the difference between learning casually and incidentally from our experiences, and learning deliberately from them. Praxis also involves the relationship between theory and practice, enabling us to develop new theories for practice in the future, based on our practical experiences in the past (Figure 5.6).

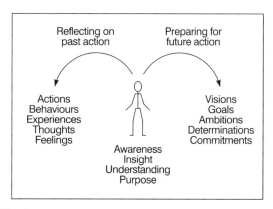

*Figure 5.6* Praxis

Working with these concepts enables us to see that review and evaluation are not only about testing and measurement, but more essentially about understanding. As managers we need to develop a powerful predisposition to this more reflective and enquiring approach. As reviewers and evaluators we are seeking to understand how organizational purposes drive actions, and the effects those actions have on the various participants in school life. Praxis is the process we engage in to seek to understand those effects.

Dialogue is the vital collaborative activity which provides information and insight that can be used to identify and guide future developments. It enables us to build that most important resource – *organizational intelligence*. To really know what is going on in a school we need to talk to people and listen carefully to their experiences. Virtually all the information needed by an organization to improve itself is already within it – in the hearts and minds of all those involved. Dialogue can be the powerful means by which we gather and accumulate this information and make it available to all concerned.

### Praxis and the evolutionary crisis

Praxis is perhaps the only useful means we have at our disposal to confront the unprecedented pressures that have created the evolutionary crisis in human affairs. Praxis is the opposite of panic, and a creative alternative to the over-hurried and sometimes desperate decision-making that we can find ourselves resorting to so often.

One of the effects of these various pressures and demands is an increase in our workload and this generates a compulsion to work harder and longer than is really good for us. The paradoxical solution is that we will have to slow down in order to speed up. Often it is the fear of failure, and the anticipation of shame and guilt, that drives us so relentlessly forward. It is not so much the work itself that is difficult as the psychological pain and distress we experience when we realize we may not be coping, and the gap between what we are supposed to do and what we are able to do comfortably seems to widen inexorably.

---

*Box 5.10*
*Future shock*
This condition of inner turmoil was referred to by Alvin Toffler (1971) as future shock – a disorientation in human sensibility created by change which moves faster than our capacity to adapt to it comfortably. It is also referred to by some as existential angst – a deep and disturbing discontent with the way things are. Whatever we call it, many of us will recognize the feelings that so often accumulate when the pressures build up almost to breaking point. But we seem to have no choice but to battle on, putting on brave faces and struggling to ignore the nagging pain within.

---

The American writer Joanna Macy (1995) has referred to the despair that we increasingly seem to experience about the quality of our lives and our apparent incapacity to get on top of things, to get some respite from the treadmill and not to feel quite so powerless. Instead of confronting the reality we tend to put up with it, engaging occasionally in jokey banter about how terrible things are, but struggling on in our private worlds of worry and despair. Macy suggests that one problem inhibiting us from facing up to our difficulties and dilemmas is fear.

---

Box 5.11
*Existential angst*
(Macy, 1995)
There are real problems preventing us from confronting our real difficulties and concerns:

- Fear of the pain involved in really confronting how we feel.
- Fear of being considered a moaner.
- Fear of appearing unable to cope.
- Fear of the guilt we would feel by confessing.
- Fear of causing distress to others.
- Fear of appearing too emotional.
- Fear of feeling more powerless than we do.

---

Clearly our socialization and upbringing did little to prepare us for this significant evolutionary crisis.

One vital adaptational initiative to combat this conspiracy of silence is to bring our worries and concerns out into the open, to make them available more deliberately and consciously to ourselves, but also through dialogue with others. One difficulty with this is the social pressure to stoicism and acceptance in our culture – to get on with life and not to make such heavy weather of it. When people do disclose aspects of their deep discontent and despair they are often thought of as moaners, even if we recognize something of our own painful experience in what they describe. Like us we would prefer they kept it to themselves.

Something of a conceptual breakthrough is needed here if we are to break the stranglehold of this condition. By making a distinction between moaning, saying how terrible things are and how awful it is to be a victim of other people's decisions, and confronting, facing up to the realities of our circumstances and accepting our own share of responsibility for them, we may discover a creative way forward.

As managers we have a vital role in leading this conceptual shift. We will need to create opportunities for colleagues to address and confront the realities of the pressures they experience at work and the painful and debilitating effects these can have. Occupational stress is an organizational issue, created in the workplace, and increased by overbearing and insensitive managers. Perhaps it is the managers themselves who initially have the most to gain from confronting and disclosing the complex dynamics of their own pressures and stresses.

As schools, like all other organizations, seek ways to adapt to changing times and fresh pressures, they will need to have practical as well as conceptual ways to break the traditional mould. This will involve the introduction of more formal procedures to help participants in school life – pupils as well as teachers – to deal with the inner experiences of their work. Praxis needs to become a working methodology for managing life in schools. For teachers this will mean new uses for staff meetings, appraisal, mentoring and school development planning. When we are faced with a major adaptational breakdown then only radical measures will do.

In practical terms it will mean the cultivation of what might be called *the process agenda* – a deliberate focusing on how we feel and think about our work and the ways that the management of our roles and responsibilities is affecting us physically, emotionally and psychologically. New skills and techniques borrowed from counselling and therapeutic practice will be necessary if we are to enable ourselves to develop the inner strength to find the optimism and commitment that our crucial roles in schools will demand.

Macy suggests that our preparedness to acknowledge our inner pains and pressures, and indeed to disclose our most heartfelt hopes and ambitions, is a measure of our caring. Engaging with colleagues in examinations and explorations of these inner dimensions of work will have considerable benefits. It will help us to:

- perceive more clearly the crisis confronting us
- feel more connected and less alone with our worries and concerns
- be relieved of the pressure and falseness of our pretence that things are OK
- feel bolder to face the challenges ahead.

---

*Box 5.12*
*Adaptational empowerment*
(Macy, 1995)
Five principles to support adaptational empowerment:

1 Feelings of emotional and psychological pain are natural and healthy.
2 These feelings are only dysfunctional if kept hidden and denied.
3 Information about external reality is not enough, we need to focus on the inner dimensions of our lives.
4 Unblocking repressed feelings releases energy and clears the mind.
5 Unblocking our pain reconnects us to the larger web of life, taking away some of our isolation from each other.

---

There is major work here for school managers and leaders. Staff welfare and well-being has to be placed in a much wider context than good physical conditions for work and appropriate remuneration. The presence of a *feel bad factor* is an almost unbearable cost for an organization with such a vital role to play in our society.

---

Box 5.13
*Adaptational praxis*
The processes of action and reflection, dialogue and process review will play a vital part in bringing about some much needed shifts in the dynamics of work:

separateness  →  connectedness
individualism  →  community
privacy          →  openness

Cultures of separateness, individualism and privacy tend to create organizational pathologies which can seriously undermine effort and achievement. New cultures of connectedness, community and openness are urgently needed if we are to encourage our schools to become the life enhancing and enriching organizations they have the potential to be.

---

This approach is not an easy option, if it were we would have discovered it long ago. But it is an urgent one. These turbulent times demand change – not so much at the outer level where almost all attention is focused, but at the inner level where stress and breakdown are the current adaptational responses. There has to be a better way.

This discussion about praxis has been placed in this chapter because it is essentially concerned with the gaining of insight and understanding. Reflective practice has become one of the central ideas in the development of learning organizations and its processes have practical applications in all areas of school life. While it is not within the scope of this book to consider it further, we must note in passing that praxis is a tool for learning. We have considered it in the service of school management. We must also appreciate that it is a tool for the pupils themselves.

- Review your own reflective practice in the light of Freire's theory (Figure 5.5).
- How do you handle your own experiences of pressure and stress?
- What practical steps could you take as a manager to encourage the conceptual shift from moaning to confronting?

# 6 Organizational life

There has to be some kind of educational process bringing the art of living into day to day management. There has always been a complete difference between the way individuals relate to their colleagues in business, and the way that they relate to their friends and family. In the latter area, kindness and tolerance are not regarded as sentimental and wet, but as making the relationship work. Can one parallel this in business now? The difference between the two sets of attitudes is beginning to narrow and that may be the answer to tomorrow's problems.
(Kinsman, 1983)

## Introduction

The last three chapters have focused on the three strategic elements introduced in the organizational model illustrated in Chapter 2 (Figure 2.4). High-quality strategic management is crucial if the school is to realize its ambitions and provide the best possible services to its pupils. The organizational model also emphasizes the cultural dimension of the school – the human climate within which the strategic work is conducted. How we relate to each other at work and how we are managed and treated can significantly affect our attitudes to work and the levels of commitment and energy we are prepared to release. It is to these aspects of organizational life that we now turn.

This chapter will:

- outline the significant elements of organizational culture
- highlight the importance we should attach to the inner worlds of our pupils and colleagues
- explore the factors which affect our levels of energy and commitment at work
- examine the dynamics of entropic and syntropic organizational cultures.

## The significance of organizational culture

The concept of culture can apply to any sort of human group, from the nation-state at one end, to the nuclear family at the other. Schools like most business organizations exhibit the following characteristics:

1 They are consciously established to marshal social power.
2 They are driven by relatively explicit goals.
3 They are composed of functional positions, roles that are distinct from the individuals occupying them.
4 They have explicit rules which govern the relationships between the roles.

As organizations underwent fast change during the Industrial Revolution, it was necessary to lay down principles for their efficient management. Many of these became crystallized into the notion of bureaucracy. This is a way of managing an organization which places significant emphasis upon:

- written rules
- a hierarchy of roles
- defined functions
- staffing by waged and salaried persons.

What happened during this process of bureaucratization was that workers became increasingly subordinated to the systems and procedures, establishing the principle that staff exist to serve the bureaucratic structures, and that formal structure is needed to manage the work of staff.

One of the most dangerous and debilitating outcomes of treating organizations as machines has been the denial of the essential complexities, ambiguities and paradoxes which are inherently present when any group of people set to work in a collective setting. The people who work in organizations have become victims of a rational approach to a non-rational phenomenon.

Once we accept that organizations do not behave only in rational ways, we open up new realms of interest, excitement, opportunity and possibility. In the historical time-scale of our species, work organizations are a relatively recent phenomenon, and we still have a great deal to learn about how they work and what governs their complexity and volatility.

As a society we raise enormous expectations of our institutions and organizations, and yet we are surprised when they do not work. Given their designs, and many of the inherited assumptions about how people in them should be treated, we should be amazed that they work at all! In reality, organizations are rich in intrigue, mystery, passion, confusion, double-dealing and resentment. They have a high tolerance of complexity yet often behave in bizarre ways when under pressure.

It is this last characteristic which has been at the heart of the problem. A great deal of traditional management and leadership theory has been developed on the assumption that work organizations do not have to be designed as places conducive to human activity, but as well ordered machines. If we view workers as the necessary but passive parts of a complex mechanism, then we tend to construct an approach to organizational life which is essentially mechanistic.

*Box 6.1*
*Characteristics of human culture*
The cultural anthropologists Hicks and Gwynne (1990) outline seven characteristics of human culture:

1 Collective
2 Shared
3 Compulsory
4 Social
5 Integrative
6 Dynamic
7 Unique to humans.

One of the keys to the successful management of change is a sensitive attention to cultural factors. Essentially this means trying to make sense of why people behave as they do; the extent to which their behaviour is culturally determined and the ways in which culture can be deliberately built and developed in ways that optimize the organizational purposes. Some cultures are implicitly stability prone – struggling to maintain the *status quo* in the face of demand and expectation for change. Others are stability phobic – anxious to avoid any sense of sameness or complacency. Most organizations find themselves somewhere between these two extremes.

One attempt to provide a model of organizational culture has been provided by Johnson and Scholes (1989). Figure 6.1 outlines the

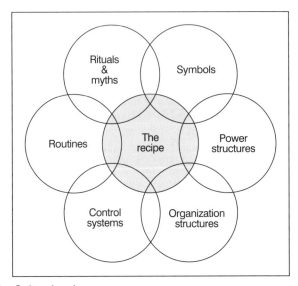

*Figure 6.1* Cultural web

components of what they describe as the *cultural web*. Johnson and Scholes build their model around the idea of the *recipe* – the sum total of beliefs, assumptions and behaviours which form the culture of an organization.The six elements combine to preserve and sustain the recipe in relation to changing environmental forces. The recipe, either consciously or unconsciously, is a major force in determining both policy and strategy.

While this model gives us a map to inform and assist our thinking and understanding of organizational life, it tends to focus on functions and attributes. A further set of factors is now outlined. These place more emphasis on how participants actually experience life at work and the ways they internalize those experiences which determine their behaviour.

The following features of organizational culture provide us with a framework to examine the crucial human factors in management and leadership:

- assembly
- organization
- contract
- role
- management
- hierarchy
- trust and control
- relationships
- needs and aspirations
- community.

## Assembly

Distinctive human cultures tend to be created whenever a group or groups of people come together on a regular basis. This coming together is not only necessary in order to serve organizational needs, it is also a key factor in determining the organization's attitudinal landscape, and in creating behavioural mores which can significantly affect the success or otherwise of the organization itself. Through the process of assembly co-workers share experiences, transact business, build relationships, make decisions, pick up new ideas, give and receive support, react to others in the hierarchical structure and strive to bring meaning to their organizational experiences.

Sometimes assembly can be structured to build common purpose and develop organizational cohesion. In schools, assembly is the only means by which pupils and teachers can experience themselves as a whole organization. Staff meetings serve to co-ordinate professional activity, to iron out confusions and uncertainties and to provide a forum for consultation and collaboration. A great deal of assembly is casual and incidental – meeting people in corridors, conversing in coffee breaks and the social interaction before and after formal occasions.

### Organization

Organization implies assembly for specified purposes and the application of rules, procedures and regulations for the conduct of the organization's business. An organization succeeds or fails by the extent to which these organizational procedures create efficiency and effectiveness, enabling the organization to meet its targets within its resource limitations. A key part of organizational life is carrying out the organizational tasks that are required.

### Contract

People work in organizations on the basis of a contract of employment. This is a legally binding agreement of mutual benefit through which we receive financial and other benefits in return for carrying out specified roles and responsibilities to an appropriate standard. Employment legislation has become sophisticated in recent years to protect both employees rights, and to clarify how disputes and grievances should be managed within a framework of accountability.

### Role

Most employees are contracted on the basis of a particular role or type of work. This role raises both requirements and expectations on the worker, and indicates the boundaries of the job and the limits of authority and responsibility within it. In some organizations role conflict occurs because these boundaries are insufficiently defined, or members of the organization are not well informed about the details of each other's role.

### Management

Once an organization has more than a handful of members it is usually necessary to create management roles. These are special roles, concerned not so much with the primary tasks of the organization, as with organizing the work of those who do carry out the primary tasks. In small voluntary organizations it is usual to find such management roles as chair, secretary and treasurer. In business organizations the head is usually defined as chief executive or managing director and specialist units or subdivisions of the organization are managed by heads of department.

### Hierarchy

Roles and responsibilities have traditionally been organized in levels, with the most powerful and highly paid at the top, and the least powerful and most lowly paid at the bottom. Traditionally, hierarchies have operated on the belief that work has to be tightly supervised, particularly at the lower levels, and that people cannot be trusted to work in self-directed and self-regulating ways.

## Trust and control

The dynamics of trust and control are crucial factors in the culture of any organization, and were discussed in Chapter 4. A key question for management and leadership is to balance these two vital forces to create optimum energy and commitment. One of the harmful inherited traditions of organizational life is the assumption that workers cannot be trusted, and therefore have to be tightly controlled and supervised. Yet one of the factors that has been found to be most demotivating and stifling of initiative and enterprise in organizations is the presence of over-controlling supervision.

## Relationships

Organizations involve people in working together. Becoming part of a collaborative enterprise is a very important element in most people's lives, and the opportunity to make friends and to forge partnerships serves a very basic human need. Good organizations recognize this and build their organizational cultures accordingly. Others try and inhibit relationships, believing that people will tend to serve their own personal interests at the expense of the organization.

## Need and aspirations

Human beings are a needy species. We are also ambitious for ourselves, often setting challenging targets for our lives. Commitment to an organization often depends upon the extent to which the work satisfies the pattern of needs and aspirations we bring with us to work each day. Increasingly, management theory is placing an important emphasis on the need to link individuals' needs and aspirations to their roles and responsibilities, on the basis that the more people experience success and satisfaction in their work, the greater will be their desire to take on new challenges and increase their responsibilities.

## Community

Being part of a successful and cohesive community is very important to most of us and we tend to judge the quality of our work organizations by the extent to which we feel and experience this sense of togetherness, collaboration and interdependence through our work.

---

*Box 6.2*
*Cultural metaphors*
A distinctive insight into organizational life is provided by Gareth Morgan (1986). He outlines the sorts of metaphors that people have used to describe the organizations they work in:

- organizations as machines
- organizations as organisms
- organizations as brains
- organizations as political systems
- organizations as instruments of domination
- organizations as flux and transformation
- organizations as psychic prisons
- organizations as culture.

When people use metaphors such as these, we gain valuable insights into how they perceive and experience life at work, and how those perceptions and experiences affect the quality of their work.

---

These eight metaphors can be used very effectively to illuminate our understanding of our organization's culture. By posing the following question for each of the metaphors we can generate a whole variety of data that will provide rich material for analysis: In what ways does this school behave like a machine?

Organizational cultures are ecologies within which the social, phenomenological and interpersonal complexities of the school are worked out. A number of significant features of modern organizational cultures can be noted:

- the richness of personal experience represented in them
- the messiness of events and incidents
- an uncertainty about tomorrow
- disorder despite efforts at organizational tidiness
- fun and enjoyment in daily life
- enthusiasm and excitement.

A wide range of factors and components combine to create an organizational culture. The following list is by no means comprehensive, but it does serve to emphasize the range and complexity of the many elements that affect our lives at work:

- people telling the stories of their life
- people telling stories about the organization
- language, both personal and professional

Box 6.3
*Culture and understanding*
Peter Anthony (1994) has suggested that it is through an understanding of the culture of the organization that participants are able to bring meaning to the daily experience of their work:

> Cultures may provide the basic,
> theoretical and perceptual building
> processes upon which we rely to
> organize our inchoate experience.

- shared experience
- sense of commonality
- taken for grantedness
- the power of traditions
- daily incidents and events
- shared meanings and understandings
- power and authority
- professional ambiguities
- conflicts over ideology
- moral dilemmas
- interpersonal perceptions and assumptions.

All of these complex issues are in a constant state of flux, changing and adapting over time. This means that culture is both a temporary phenomenon, never fixed and always changing, but also a continuous feature of school life. There is always a culture, but we are never ever really sure what state it is in at any one time.

- What would you hightlight as the significant features of the organizational culture of your school?
- Use the Johnson and Scholes model (Figure 6.1) to generate a cultural recipe for your school.
- Try the exercise based on Gareth Morgan's cultural metaphors.

## Human experience

Management theory has been slow to accept that human experience lies at the heart of organizational culture and is one of the most crucial factors in determining an organization's successes and failures. If we think of culture in the climatological sense, then we can appreciate that certain climate patterns and types of weather are unconducive to the work that learners and teachers do in schools. Unlike actual climate patterns, however, organizational climate is created by the organization itself, particularly by those who manage and lead it. People are just as sensitive to these organizational climate patterns as they are to the actual weather, which features so prominently in our personal conversations.

In attempting to understand the complex nature of any organizational culture it is important to understand the complex duality of inner and outer worlds (Figure 6.2).

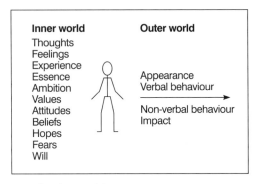

**Inner world**

Thoughts
Feelings
Experience
Essence
Ambition
Values
Attitudes
Beliefs
Hopes
Fears
Will

**Outer world**

Appearance
Verbal behaviour

Non-verbal behaviour
Impact

*Figure 6.2* Inner and outer worlds

One way to understand a school is to observe it, to notice what happens in it, how people behave – what they do and what they say, and the effects that these actions have on others. We can notice the structures that exist, the procedures that are established and the outcomes that are achieved through all this work. This is what school inspectors focus on and make judgements about – the visible and tangible work of the school. The inner world is not so visible, audible or tangible. It is the world that exists within the hearts and minds of each member of the organization. It includes all that we experience, think about, feel and are affected by moment to moment throughout each school day. It also includes the ways we construct the meaning of these disparate experiences, and the conclusions we come to about our own work, the contributions of others and the quality of the organization as a whole.

In the struggle to make organizations work efficiently, and with optimum control, managers in the past regarded their workers as machines which could be made efficient by design, supervision and control. So the inner worlds of workers were regarded as insignificant to the determination of effectiveness. Only in recent years have we begun to realize the terrible consequences of this narrow view of human behaviour. Deliberate attention to the culture of the organization is the way we can begin to restore a proper balance to management and leadership, and help to make it the truly creative and transforming work it needs to be.

So these many different and distinctive inner worlds are key factors in determining commitment, effort, effectiveness and success. It cannot be good for any organization to have people in it who are depressed by their experience of life at work. It must be in the best interests of a school that its managers work imaginatively and creatively to make learning interesting and enriching for the pupils, and to make the teaching deeply satisfying for the staff.

Central to this demanding and complex challenge is an under-standing of the nature of human potential. This was referred to in Chapter 3 where the concept of the *directional tendency* was referred to. Leaders and managers need to embrace this significant idea.

---

*Box 6.4*
*Human potential*
(Evans and Russell, 1990)
The following propositions have been outlined by Willis Harman:

- The potentialities of the individual human being are far greater than current assumptions about the person would lead us to believe.
- A far greater proportion of significant human experience that we normally assume is comprised of unconscious processes, particularly those involving such areas of experience as intuition and creativity.
- Images of the self, which can be positive or negative, play a predominant role in limiting or enhancing the actualization of one's potentialities.

---

In other words, it is through the inner worlds of learners and teachers that many of the keys to school effectiveness lie. If we choose to underestimate their significance, or to ignore their presence, then we are unlikely to be able to create the conditions conducive to releasing the creativity, imagination and energy that a successful school depends upon.

---

- To what extent do you accept the view that an understanding of, and attention to, the inner worlds of our colleagues is a proper concern for managers?
- How does your own management style reflect your position on this issue?

# Work and well-being

In determining the guiding principles for our leadership and management work, it is important to reflect on our own experiences of organizational life.

Consider the following words and reflect on any organizational experiences they evoke for you.

conflict    accepted    ignored    encouraged

supported    misunderstood    oppressed    frustrated

prized    anger    abused    involved    cajoled

trusted    appreciated    resentment    excluded

guilt    fun    listened to    excitement    valued

criticized    humiliated    reprimanded    embarrassed

accused    rejected

Draw a ring around words that evoke memories of particular incidents and events at work. Try to recall how you felt at the time and the circumstances that gave rise to those feelings.

What we are likely to discover from this exercise is that the work we do, and the way we do it, is significantly affected by our experience. When we have been treated in ways which make us feel good about who we are and what we have done, then our commitment is likely to have risen, along with our energy and enthusiasm. If we have been treated badly, then the consequent feelings of anger, resentment, humiliation or embarrassment are likely to decrease our sense of commitment, making us more cautious and defensive. Figure 6.3 outlines this phenomenon.

During much of our time at work we tend to experience various levels of satisfaction. We reach the end of the day feeling neither highly fulfilled nor desperately unhappy. From time to time however we have experiences which either lift us beyond satisfaction or send us below dissatisfaction. Whatever the movement, it is likely to affect our

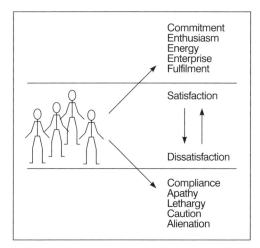

*Figure 6.3* Work and well-being

relationship to our work, the organization itself and to our levels of commitment and energy.

Working deliberately to build and develop a positive, friendly, enriching and ambitious organizational culture is the way we strive to create the possibilities illustrated by the upward movement in the diagram. Few organizations will ever achieve a consistency of success in this, but many will be able to create conditions for positive growth and development and work unceasingly to avoid the terrible consequences of the downward movement.

Our capacity to work effectively towards the goals of the organization is determined by a variety of factors. Investigations into what people tend to desire for themselves at work suggest that:

- We want to feel a sense of satisfaction, both about the work we do and about its contribution to organization itself.
- We want to feel able to exercise preferences, both about the conduct of our own roles and responsibilities, but also in decisions about organizational direction and practice.
- We want to feel interested in, and concerned about, our work so that our efforts and contributions are in tune with our purposes in life.
- We want to feel challenged to use our best abilities to achieve worthwhile goals.
- We want to enjoy the process of work and to experience pleasure in being part of the organizational enterprise.

Professional work tends to afford a good deal of autonomy, but much will depend upon how autonomy is perceived and experienced by each member of staff. We can easily regard those who are in posts senior to our own as having a power/coercive relationship with us, thereby having the right and authority to inhibit, deny and limit the

---

*Box 6.5*
*Job satisfaction*
(Hackman and Lawler, 1971)
Four key variables have been discovered to be particularly significant in creating a sense of job satisfaction:

- *Variety* The degree to which a job offers variety of tasks and activities through a range of processes.
- *Autonomy* The extent to which we have a say in organizing our own role and determining the approaches and processes to be used.
- *Identity* The extent to which we and others can identify the significant contributions we make.
- *Feedback* The extent to which we receive information about our work and its contribution to the organization.

---

freedom we crave. If we feel that the way we are treated at work is unreasonably inhibiting of freedom then there are significant consequences. Our relationships with senior colleagues can become a struggle to protect, defend and fight for more freedom and autonomy, which in turn can increase their determination to maintain their status and authority by further trying to limit and control us.

We do have choices:

- to accept the *status quo* and give up the struggle
- to work subversively to undermine the *status quo*
- to act openly to transform the *status quo*.

One thing is certain – some of our potential energy, available for the work within the role, will be transferred to the struggle, with dangerous consequences for our own effectiveness, and for the interests of the school as a whole.

A major issue for many managers is that of the commitment levels of their colleagues. In schools we are also familiar with this in terms of pupils' commitment levels. Many managers talk about a *lack of commitment* as if it were some generalized commodity. We become committed when we identify strongly with a cause or a worthwhile purpose. Commitment tends to be high in organizations where there are powerful causes, strong beliefs, shared values and clear visions.

In Figure 6.3 a distinction was made between commitment created when we feel interested and involved in our work, and compliance – doing the necessary work but without strong feelings of interest and involvement.

---

Box 6.6
*The commitment continuum*
Our commitment to work and to the roles and responsibilities we hold will exist somewhere on the following versions of the commitment continuum:

- commitment – scepticism – reservation – hostility
- enthusiasm – disillusionment – panic – search for the guilty – punishment of the innocent – praise and honour for the non-participants
- commitment – co-operation – support – acceptance – indifference – apathy – protest – showdown – sabotage.

---

All of us will have our own experiences of these dynamics in operation. A great deal of management work in schools is about working to encourage commitment in pupils and teachers. This can never be achieved only through exhortations and rallying cries, and hardly ever by coercive command. Managers can do much to increase commitment in others by:

- constantly noting individual and collective achievements and bringing these to everyone's attention
- making explicit the relationship between the behaviour that created the success and the specific benefits that resulted
- articulating the causes to which commitment is needed
- providing feedback on the relationship between energy expended on an activity, and the positive consequences and results achieved.

Working to build a positive organizational culture will be affected by the *inheritance factor* – traditions established in earlier regimes of the school, which can be very difficult to shift. Most organizations have an institutional memory that is inherited through the different generations. Staffroom stories are told about *the old days*, truths are embellished and myths are perpetuated. People tend not to forget the past and can harbour it with some relish, resurrecting it when a point needs to be made or a painful reminder used to sway an argument. This is particularly so when change is on the agenda, when previous failures are used to warn against the dangers of over-hasty innovation. This can sometimes lead an organization to resist necessary change, and become reluctant to engage in new thinking and fresh ideas.

As we discovered from the exercise at the beginning of this section, what we bring with us from the past, both individually and collectively, can affect the way we deal with the present and the way we approach the future. This can pose considerable challenges for managers who will need to:

- reconcile new beliefs with old stories
- examine entrenched assumptions
- develop new styles and approaches
- change patterns of work and decision-making
- promote new assumptions and propositions.

One useful indicator of the state of an organizational culture is to listen for the use of the pronoun *them*. When we want to keep a distance from people we are connected with we tend to use this pronoun rather than the more inclusive *we*. In organizational life *them* can refer to:

- others either above me or below me in the hierarchy
- my particular line manager
- colleagues who do not respect me
- colleagues I dislike or disapprove of
- clients and customers.

In schools the pronoun is often used to refer to the pupils, their parents, the office, OFSTED, and those who seem to be making life harder than it need be.

---

The following questions provide a means of assessing the ways in which the organizational culture of your school may be affecting your levels of commitment and energy.

- In what ways is this organization helping me to satisfy my ambitions and aspirations for my life and work?
- In what ways is this organization helping me to participate in the direction and development of its present and its future?
- In what ways is this organization helping me to lay healthy foundations and opportunities for those who follow in my role?

---

Organizational culture is a complex phenomenon and managers can find it very baffling to try to identify the precise reasons why individuals and groups behave as they do. To gain useful insights we can turn to the world of biological cultures.

Translated to the workplace these ideas provide us with a useful theoretical model. In reality, no organization would conform to either of these extreme positions, but would exist somewhere on the continuum between the two. Neither would the cultural forces ever be static, but would create movement in either direction through mood

---

*Box 6.7*
*Syntropic and entropic cultures*
The work of biological scientists such as Ilya Prigogine (1979) and Albert Szent-Gyoergyi (1974) on syntropy and entropy in organic systems, provides a useful framework. They observed that some organic cultures have an enhancing or syntropic effect, tending to display increasing energy, order and organization. Applied to organizational cultures then these two tendencies work in opposite directions:

*Syntropic culture*
Involvement in the organization tends to increase:

● commitment
● energy
● enthusiasm
● enterprise
● responsibility
● collaboration
● initiative
● confidence.

*Entropic culture*
Involvement in the organization tends to increase:

● compliance
● apathy
● caution
● defensiveness
● alienation
● cynicism
● mistrust
● fear.

---

swings, bad days, calm periods and moments of crisis. The psychosocial landscapes of organizational cultures are the product of the human forces at work within them and include:

● power and authority structures
● rules and regulations governing staff
● attitudes of senior to junior staff
● age profiles
● status differentials
● reward and punishment systems

- patterns of rights and responsibilities
- degrees of discrimination
- management systems
- celebration and acknowledgement of success
- staff involvement in decision-making
- access to information.

Another useful way of approaching the management of organizational culture is to consider the more specific factors which create syntropy and cause entropy. Studies have shown that organizational behaviour and work performance are directly affected by the assumptions held about them by those in positions of authority and power. The enormous potential which staff and pupils bring with them to school every day tends to be activated and enhanced when senior staff believe in that potential, and seek ways to foster its energetic release. This potential can also be thwarted and frustrated if senior staff believe that effective performance will only be achieved through rigid supervision and tight control. When these assumptions are translated into management behaviour then either they tend to operate like nutrients, enhancing the potential of others, or toxins, crushing and inhibiting that potential.

## Entropic cultures

Among the many toxins that can work so powerfully to inhibit our potential are those verbal and non-verbal behaviours which activate particular emotions such as fear, anger, resentment and jealousy. Such painful feelings can be stimulated when we are on the receiving end of particular types of communication behaviour:

- having our ideas rejected or stolen
- facing constant, carping criticism
- being ignored
- being judged
- being over-directed
- not being listened to
- being misunderstood.

Such behaviours happen occasionally in most organizations, but when they are employed consistently and systematically they can seriously undermine self-esteem, confidence, commitment and professional ambition.

A major cultural issue in many organizations is that of conflict. We tend to work with the misplaced belief that because we have worked with someone for a long time we know them.

---

*Box 6.8*
*The iceberg theory*
Just as only about 10 per cent of an iceberg is above the waterline, so in organizations only about 10 per cent of what really matters about people and their relationships is available for us to see and hear.

Above the water level people seem to relate in polite and friendly ways, but below the water level are great psychological and emotional collisions. Negative emotions such as resentment, anger, jealousy and guilt tend to be concealed in everyday encounters. The difficulties are increased when it is the hierarchy who are responsible for these deep feelings in the first place. Many of us do not want to exacerbate the problem by confronting it, thereby deepening the resentment and making us more withdrawn and undisclosing.

---

Hostility and conflict is often aroused when particular individuals feel oppressed – pupils by their teachers, for example, or staff by their senior colleagues. When personal and professional values are attacked we can often feel it is our personalities rather than our work which is being criticized. We tend to hold in the painful feelings we experience because we feel ashamed that we can attract such hostility.

Effective cultural management involves creating positive ways to handle hostility and conflict. A first step is to accept the inevitability of conflict. Given the fact that great issues of educational philosophy and ideology are being played out each day in schools, it is not surprising that disagreements occur, or that professional stances are challenged. We need to build a set of assumptions about the nature of conflict in schools:

- Conflict is a natural feature of human relationships.
- Accepting conflict as natural and necessary is an important step in establishing firm cultural foundations.
- Conflicts create new opportunities to resolve differences and misunderstandings.
- Conflicts need to be understood in terms of individual behaviour, needs and motivation, and organizational dynamics and politics.

Striving for integration sums up the very essence of the cultural dimension in management work. It may take a lot of painstaking and sensitive work, but there really is no alternative if we are to optimize the enormous aptitudes and potentialities of our pupils and colleagues. It is a complex process of recognizing the inner world of thoughts, feelings, experiences, hopes and fears, and realizing this is the raw material for the effective leader's work.

*Box 6.9*
*Managing conflict*
John Rowan (1992) suggests there are only three possibilities:

*Domination*
One side wins and the other loses. This often leads to the losing side trying to build up its forces so that it can win next time round. It perpetuates, or even sets in motion, a win–lose relationship of low synergy.

*Compromise*
Each side gives up part of what it wants for the sake of peace. This is always unsatisfying to some degree, and each side may try to get its missing bit in some overt or covert way.

*Integration*
Both sides get what they really wanted. This may need quite a bit of work to see what it is that each side did really want. Another way of putting this is to say that we need to look behind the wants.

This third way, integration, where it can be found, is the most satisfying.

Of particular significance are those behaviours which tend to arise out of a traditional preoccupation with sharply differentiated organizational hierarchies. When management behaviour reinforces status separation, then those lower down the hierarchical triangle can experience a range of painful and inhibiting feelings:

- a sense of inadequacy
- inability to express oneself
- inability to influence anyone
- feelings of being shut out
- increase in cynicism
- increase in destructive feelings
- feelings that one has either to dominate or be dominated
- feeling that to conform is the best thing
- feeling that intolerance and oppression have to be accepted
- feeling that new ideas can only come from the top
- feeling that there is no way to communicate with those at the top.

Another major factor in determining the characteristics of an organization's culture arises out of the assumptions held by senior staff about those lower in the hierarchy. Figure 6.4 illustrates two distinct positions.

Box 6.10
*Cultural pathologies*
(Argyris, 1960)
As long ago as 1960, in his pioneering work on organizational behaviour, Chris Argyris coined the phrase *cultural pathologies* to describe such entropic characteristics as dependence, compliance, resistance, complacency, inhibition, depression and resentment. He claimed that when these were constantly present in the members of organizations, then their potential to give of their best was significantly reduced.

There are still far too many organizations where these pathologies continue to apply.

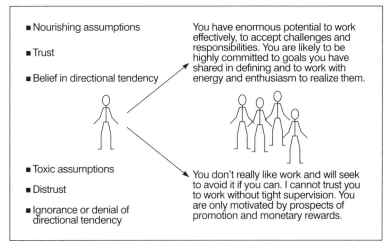

*Figure 6.4*  Managers' assumptions about workers

What we do know from a range of research studies (Kennedy, 1991; Pugh and Hickson, 1989) is that if we assume that our colleagues and pupils will not want to work effectively and are unable to do so without our forceful supervision and control, then we must not be surprised if they return this attempt at superiority and domination with apathy and compliance. Such life-diminishing assumptions seem to have a multiplying effect, spreading throughout the organization and holding everyone in its thrall.

It must be in the school's interest to develop the potential that everybody brings with them each day. Yet far too often this potential is inhibited and sometimes almost crushed. Argyris (1973) has suggested that this often happens in organizations because managers are hampered by their own inherited beliefs about needing to be dominant, and lack both trust in the individual's potential to flourish, and the interpersonal confidence to encourage it.

---

*Box 6.11*
*Toxic management*
(Argyris, 1973)
Argyris highlights three key toxins that have the effect of stifling potential:

- By concentrating their efforts on the management of tasks, managers have an excuse for not taking a sensitive interest in workers' needs, concerns, pressures and stresses.
- Managers display an obsession with rationality and thinking which results in feelings being played down and regarded as insignificant. This denigrates the quality of interpersonal needs and relationships, which are viewed as marginal to effectiveness and not real work.
- Managers believe and act with a strong adherence to the *chain of command* principle, believing that human relations are most effectively influenced through unilateral direction, coercion and control, as well as through token rewards and punishments.

---

Although such managers are loyal, hard working and dedicated, the effect of their approaches is to discourage risk-taking, openness, the expression of feelings and the development of cohesive and trusting relationships. Clearly there is much work to be done in building both more life-enhancing assumptions about those we work with, and in developing an interpersonal style which recognizes and respects the vital significance of the inner dimensions of people's lives.

---

*Box 6.12*
*Toxic psychology*
David Krueger (1992) has observed that some of the worst hazards for workers in an organization are not machines and substances but the toxic psychology of those operating the systems and structures. These toxins arise, he suggests, from:

- boredom with the work
- lack of influence and power
- absence of recognition
- over-control and supervision.

---

A particular challenge for schools is what we might call *system dissonance*. This is a situation in an organization where rules are made for one level of activity but not for others. In schools this would be characterized by having different assumptions about staff and pupils.

Fullan and Hargreaves (1992) believe that most staff in schools are having less and less satisfying careers and that most pupils find schools less than exciting and useful places to be in. These two things they say – the lives of the educators and the lives of the teachers – are intimately related. Fullan and Hargreaves (1992) quote Sarason (1990) as saying: 'for our schools to do better than they do we have to give up the belief that it is possible to create the conditions for effective learning when those conditions do not exist for educational personnel'.

What schools need then is a culture which unifies both staff and pupils within a powerful set of purposes, aspirations and commitments.

Part of our organizational history has been the sustaining of a tradition that those who run organizations need to see the human spirit as their enemy, rather than as their most awesome ally. The psychologist David Smail (1987) notes the extent to which the exploitation of people has become endemic in organizations. He suggests that because so much of this exploitation is dishonourable, we hide its nature from ourselves. He urges a drastic shift in assumptions: 'Far from being repairable machines, human beings are embodied organisms on which damage will at least leave a scar. We simply cannot get away with using and abusing each other as we do' (Smail, 1987).

An index search through a collection of books on management and leadership found frequent references to such items as – strategy, competitive edge, team-building, market forces, innovation, customer service, quality control and delegation. It is interesting to note how few references there were, even in books with sections on organizational culture, to such items as – community, justice, ethics, fear, oppression, happiness, fun, love and affection.

## Syntropic cultures

Among the many nutrients that can act effectively to enhance human potential in schools are those verbal and non-verbal behaviours which arouse positive and pleasurable emotions such as excitement, joy, delight, happiness and affection. Such emotions can be stimulated when we are on the receiving end of particular types of communication behaviour:

- being valued
- being encouraged
- being noticed
- being trusted
- being listened to
- being respected.

The essence of effective leadership is helping people to be as effective as they themselves would like to be. This involves supporting people to release their talents and abilities from self restriction and encouraging them through positive attitudes and behaviours.

Gerard Egan (1977) has highlighted the following stances towards others as being particularly nourishing:

- Being there *for* others. This involves showing an interest in others, sharing in their successes.
- Being attentive. Listening with care and attentiveness to the other person, being prepared to give time to them. It involves commenting on those things that others do that give us satisfaction and pleasure, and offering support when things seem to be difficult.
- Co-operation. Being prepared to work alongside others, to seek their support as well as to offer our own. It also involves showing enjoyment of other people's skills and contributions in collaborative ventures.
- Regard for individuality. Accepting and valuing the fact that we are all different and that we tackle things in different ways. Not expecting others to be like us.
- Regard for autonomy. Respecting that others know their own experience best and are capable of taking responsibility for themselves. Avoiding the tendency to dominate and control.
- Assuming goodwill. Recognizing that few people in organizations are consistently motivated by maliciousness. Most of us want to do our best and feel effective and valuable. Because we do not always like what other people do does not mean that they intended to upset us.
- Understanding. Spending time with people, watching what they do and listening to what they say. Working to appreciate and understand their point of view.
- Warmth. Being sensitive and considerate to others. Conveying a sense of caring about what other people are doing and how they feel.
- Support and encouragement. Being aware of other people's needs and demonstrating a willingness to help them. Showing appreciation of what others do and an interest in the tasks they are currently engaged in.
- Genuineness. Contrary to much of our socialization it is a major sign of respect to show yourself to others as you really are.

One feature of organizational life not often focused on in management training, nor in the literature, is that of fun. For too long in this country there has been a damaging assumption that fun must imply the absence of rigour and a lack of gravitas. Having fun usually means our energy levels are higher and our commitment to what we are doing more activated. Managers need to lead by example, building a shared belief that a fun-focused school can also be a highly achieving one.

It is a tragedy that for many people, the job they really want is not the one they are currently doing. For some of us, promotion and career change is more about leaving what we are familiar with, than moving to something new. In a profession where career development is not as simple as it once seemed to be, we need to think how we can help colleagues to make their jobs as exciting, interesting, absorbing and fulfilling as possible.

The art of building and maintaining a syntropic management culture depends upon the style of leadership adopted by all of us who have management responsibilities. It is especially important that we see the major part of our role as working to satisfy the complex pattern of personal and professional needs colleagues bring with them to school every day.

|  | Positive experience | Negative experience |
|---|---|---|
| Inclusion | I feel involved, included and a key part of things | I feel shut out, ignored and excluded |
| Affection | I feel liked, valued and appreciated | I feel disliked and undervalued |
| Control | I feel in control of my own roles and responsibilities | I feel controlled by others |

*Figure 6.5* Key cultural factors

Three particular factors lie at the heart of effective culture building (Figure 6.5). The cultural dimension of school life is perhaps the most important location for our leadership work. In terms of the three factors outlined in Figure 6.5 there is important work to do:

*Inclusion*
- Helping colleagues, particularly newly appointed ones, to become known.
- Seeking opinions, asking questions, initiating dialogue, bringing task groups together.
- Providing feedback when colleagues do valuable work.
- Building networks, passing information and putting colleagues in touch with each other.

*Affection*
- Taking opportunities to meet, greet, make contact.
- Showing our pleasure and delight when colleagues are successful.
- Showing sensitive understanding when colleagues are in difficulties.

- Taking an interest in colleagues' circumstances.
- Offering help and support where appropriate.

*Control*

- Seeking to understand each colleague's experience of the control factor.
- Raising the control issue at meetings and in discussions.
- Tuning in to the micro-politics of the organization.
- Inviting feedback about systems and procedures.
- Involving colleagues into the design and implementation of changes involving them.

Each of these factors is crucially important in the high-pressure circumstances of the present, and will become increasingly significant as schools continue to break new ground into the future. Unless hard-pressed staff feel a powerful sense of belonging to the school, and a feeling of involvement in its development, they are unlikely to feel sufficiently supported to give of their best. It is also important to recognize that while school effectiveness does not depend upon everyone liking each other, warmth and affection need to be part of organizational experience if trust is to be built, and psychological security established. Constant attention to issues of control will be required if schools are to avoid ignoring crucial cultural dynamics and reinforcing the toxins that can be so destructive.

While good schools tend to be strong on affection and inclusion, there is often room for development in relation to the control factor. A tradition of strong leadership through the role of the headteacher has sometimes made it difficult for responsibilities to be spread through-out the whole staff. If we are to create more genuinely co-managing organizations then this issue has to be confronted.

In the building of a strong and nourishing organizational culture, leadership becomes a process of interacting with colleagues in ways that help to satisfy their felt needs of the moment. Leadership is subtle work, and has developed radically in most schools from the command and control styles of earlier generations. Now it is not so much a case of who is a leader and who is not, but how each of us can effectively exercise that leadership aspect of our role, and how we can offer leadership in a whole variety of situations. In this way leadership becomes more than the exercising of status and position, it becomes a function of all those involved in the co-management of the school.

Those with specific leadership responsibilities are particularly well placed to communicate in ways that both enhance the capacity of colleagues to work effectively, and to build a climate conducive to growth and development. Effective leadership is about supporting the vast resources for self-understanding, learning and growth within each of us. These resources are more likely to be activated and released when a positive climate of psychological safety and support is created.

- Consider the issue of *cultural pathologies* (Box 6.10). What in your experience are the managerial behaviours that contribute to them?
- Use Gerard Egan's stances to review your own management style.
- Reflect on the extent to which the factors outlined in Figure 5.6 are a feature of your school.
- How would you assess the contribution you make to developing the organizational culture of your school?

# 7 Multi-layered leadership

> By design and talent we were a team of specialists, and like a team of specialists in any field, our performance depended both on individual excellence and on how well we worked together. None of us had to strain to understand that we had to complement each other's specialities; it was simply a fact, and we all tried to figure out ways to make our combination more effective.
> (Bill Russell of the Boston Celtics basketball team, quoted in Senge, 1990)

## Introduction

One of the great challenges to the new paradigm in organizational management outlined in Chapter 1 is the redefinition of the term 'leadership'. Our education and upbringing, and indeed our daily engagement with national and international news tend to equate leadership with leaders – those in powerful positions in international and institutional affairs. For those concerned to help in the development of effective leadership this has tended to create problems of definition. We have a tendency to think of leadership in terms of role and personality – that leadership can only be considered as a function of those who occupy top positions in particular institutions and organizations. This suggests that leadership is something that is only possible to carry out if you are given a position of power and authority from which to act. Certainly many of those occupying such positions do demonstrate characteristics of leadership, but there are dangers in attributing such behaviour only to those so highly placed and extending the assumption to the idea that only those so placed are able to exercise leadership.

In this chapter we will:

- examine different approaches to the structuring of leadership roles in schools
- consider the processes involved in building effective management teams
- outline a range of practical strategies to manage meetings more successfully.

## Changing concepts of leadership

Theorists have approached the issue of leadership from many angles. A common approach is to take a dozen or so outstanding leaders (by common perception) and attempt to extrapolate the characteristics they seem to have in common. This can produce a list of *power behaviours* that seem to contain the clues to success. There is little evidence to suggest that this is effective in leadership training. Another false avenue is to try and tease out what it is in the personality and experience of successful leaders that may serve to explain their skills, abilities and qualities.

- Make a list of people in history who you consider to have been great leaders. What characteristics do they have? What qualities do you believe made them great?
- Now make a list of leaders you have worked with during your life. What did the ones you admired do that so impressed you? How did those who you disliked, or felt oppressed by, behave?
- What sort of leader do you see yourself as being? By what characteristics would you like to be known?

A more productive avenue is to ask the question – what is it that enables successful organizations to succeed and thrive? What emerges is a more complex answer than simply good leadership from the top. It seems that leadership is an altogether more diffuse concept than we have traditionally come to believe, that it can be exercised at all levels within organizations and that all participants are capable of practising it in some way. By focusing only on the behaviour of senior people we run the risk of losing sight of those aspects of human behaviour in organizations that leads to effectiveness and consistently high quality.

One useful definition of leadership is behaviour that enables and assists others to achieve planned goals. This suggests that leadership might have as much to do with making helpful suggestions as to do with issuing strategic directives, as much about listening to other people's ideas as about expounding your own and as much about gentleness as about toughness. What is clear is that effectiveness in organizations depends upon leadership emerging appropriately as and when necessary. Perhaps we need to change the question from who are good leaders to what examples have you seen of colleagues demonstrating good leadership. It will only be when we observe the qualities of leadership in our daughters and sons, in the new and youngest recruits to our organizations and in the pupils that we teach, that we will really be immersing ourselves in the world of leadership. Successful school management in the future will require multiple and varied types of leadership.

One of the most significant evolutionary factors in organizations concerns the issue of hierarchies, and this was discussed in the previous chapter.

> *Box 7.1*
> *The twilight of hierarchy*
> Cleveland (1985) has suggested that what we are witnessing in the management paradigm shift is what he calls the twilight of hierarchy.
>
> Complex systems, he argues, cannot be controlled externally, since the system has an inner logic and dynamic of its own. In complex systems, control resides in the pattern of relationships that comprise the system itself.

In complex organizations like schools, attempts to manage through command and control structures are unlikely to succeed and will need to give way to more collaborative approaches. Information is the key issue. Leadership by command and control tends to work when only a few people are in the know, as in the former Soviet Union, for example. In information-rich organizations, and particularly those operated through professional staffing, the nature of control changes. Large numbers of empowered people want to make policy and to be involved in making the decisions that affect their working lives. It no longer becomes possible, or useful, to try and keep secrets. The technology of information exchange has tended to democratize knowledge and information, and it is no longer easy to keep people in the dark. In this changed organizational world, decision-making proceeds less by *orders* and more by developing a *shared sense of direction*.

One of the organizational tendencies in recent years has been to create flatter management structures – *flatarchies*. These reduce the number of differentiated pay and responsibility levels, and increase a sense of partnership and collaboration. Schools continue to have somewhat steep hierarchies which can inhibit the development of a truly collaborative approach to leadership.

We need to recognize the limitations of the hierarchical principle in management, both from the organizational culture point of view and in our efforts to create more flexible and involving approaches to leadership (Box 7.2).

In practice, heterarchical management involves structures which are continuously changing to accommodate new challenges and situations. The management structure would be constantly reconfiguring itself through a variety of teams, often small and temporary, brought into being to tackle the specific tasks and projects of the moment. Leadership roles would be designated according to need rather than depend upon seniority, thus involving everyone in the co-management and co-leadership of the school.

This concept helps us to consider some exciting departures from tradition which may help us to deal more effectively with the complexities of the fast-changing world and to create new structures

---

*Box 7.2*
*Heterarchy*
(Marshall, 1994)
Hierarchies have limitations. They become inflexible. They can create impossible expectations of designated *leaders* and unproductive dynamics of dependency and abdication of individual responsibility. As we appreciate these problems and seek to honour people's diversity in skills and viewpoints, we need alternative models.

Recognizing everyone's equal humanity is an important step, but this can create cosy norms of equal needs, skills, rights and power in all situations. This, too, is limited, denying significant differences.

In the notion of *heterarchy* I see more potential. A heterarchy has no one person or principle in command. Rather, temporary pyramids of authority form as and where appropriate in a system of mutual constraints and influences.

---

which more successfully harness the skills and qualities of all the staff team.

What we are currently witnessing in many future-focused organizations is the attempt to create structures of management and leadership which are characterized more by the acceptance of temporariness than of longevity, by possibility rather than unlikeliness, and by integration rather than exclusion. Such approaches reject the idea of singular and simple solutions to problems and proceed on the assumption that compound and complex problems will require compound and complex solutions.

---

*Box 7.3*
*Multiple perspectives*
For too long we have been plagued with a dualistic obsession in much of our thinking. Things have had to be either right or wrong, with no fuzziness, no shades of grey, no uncertainty and no confusion. Such a view of how the world works, based on eighteenth-century scientific laws and mechanistic principles, fails to appreciate the range of continuously changing variables present in almost all human activity.

Leaders must give up any beliefs they may harbour that the world is built of simple, orderly structures. Dichotomies, paradoxes, ambiguities and confusions abound. They are the real stuff of organizational life.

The future demands that we embrace complexity. Our thinking will need to accommodate not one view of any issue and its alternative – the *either/or* approach – but multiple possibilities and compound options.

---

In our leadership work we will need to be less concerned with status and authority, and more concerned with making working life at school a rich and rewarding experience for everyone. This will require us to discover the ways in which we can effectively release the often hidden and inhibited potentialities of both staff and pupils.

---

- In what ways are hierarchical principles practised in your school? What effects do they have?
- How could your school embrace the concept of *flatarchy*? What challenges would this pose to senior managers?
- In what ways could the concept of *heterarchy* offer your school some new approaches to management?

---

## The leadership co-operative

The changes brought in through legislation and regulation in recent years have meant that virtually all staff in schools have seen their job descriptions expand to accommodate an ever-increasing range of tasks and responsibilities. Most teachers are now holding portfolios of responsibility which are too large and complex for any individual to discharge effectively on their own.

The combination of pressures from increased prescriptions and heightened expectations has brought about some significant effects in schools:

- increase in the weight of individual workloads
- increase in the complexity of workloads
- too little time for too many changes
- the confusion of managing many significant changes simultaneously
- lack of time for preparation, adjustment and training
- changes that are changed again either before or during implementation
- increase in confusion, uncertainty, ambiguity, turbulence
- panic to cover the ground with insufficient attention to detail
- further erosion of professional time into personal time at the expense of individual well-being and family life.

Management structures built on individual and separated responsibility are placing disproportionate pressure on some teachers, who can feel overwhelmed by the demands placed on them and who experience painful feelings of isolation, inadequacy and panic. If left unchecked and unattended to, these can lead to both personal and professional dysfunction. The educational press reports a rapidly developing tendency among teachers, senior staff in particular, to seek early retirement due to breakdowns in health and well-being.

We need to consider whether we have now reached the limit of the usefulness of traditional management structures in schools and whether constantly changing circumstances demand the development of new systems and structures to handle the ever increasing workloads that staff in schools are facing.

Traditional management structures in both primary and secondary schools have tended to designate and distribute individual staff responsibilities on the basis of three distinct functions:

- *Curriculum* In primary schools teachers take responsibility for a subject area, co-ordinating activities, leading developments and monitoring progress. In secondary schools virtually all staff are placed within at least one subject department.
- *Phase or location* Responsibilities are for phases – upper school, Key Stage 1 for example.
- *Pupil welfare* In primary schools this tends to be incorporated in the class teaching role, but in secondary schools there is often a distinctive pastoral care system and many teachers have a tutoring responsibility.

There are two features of this traditional approach which require attention:

- *Individual focus* The necessary task work of the school is spread across all those available to undertake it. Each member of staff carries a responsibility role different from all other members of staff. This means that management work tends to be carried by individuals in isolation from each other. Each individual, within the structure of accountability, carries out their own planning, operating and reviewing.
- *Responsibility driven* Each member of staff's management role is defined in terms of responsibility – a requirement to handle a particular aspect of school life. This responsibility is open-ended, operating until either the teacher vacates the post or changes are made to the role through mutual agreement with senior colleagues. It is also open-ended in terms of demand. A subject leader would be expected to deal with all issues arising in that subject area however much or little was in focus at the time.

Although some management work is collaborative – subject departments in secondary schools and year group teams in primary schools for example – there are a number of serious difficulties with this approach:

- It creates a sense of management isolation.
- It can lead to significant task overload.

- It can result in excessive pressure and stress.
- It creates inequity across the system in that some teachers can be disproportionately challenged at particular times.
- It creates problems of self-motivation.

What we need is a structure that works to overcome these difficulties and makes the management and leadership work of a school more geared to school development and management co-operation (Figure 7.1). The work of the three members of staff at the top of the diagram is driven by an open-ended job description which continues irrespective of the pressures and demands facing a school at any one time. The three colleagues have different roles from each other and carry out much of their management work alone.

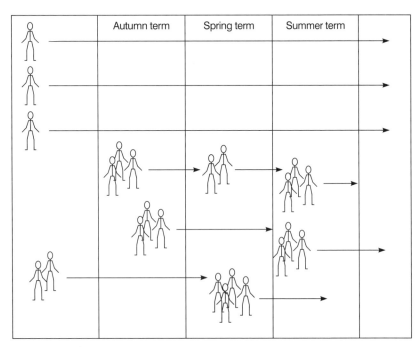

*Figure 7.1* Contrasting management structures

In the lower section the management activity of staff is driven by the school development plan for that particular year, and each member of staff joins a number of temporary teams to carry out the task work specified in the plan.

Instead of conceiving of the management task of the school as a series of functions to be supervised, it is useful to see it as a series of tasks to be undertaken within a specific time period. The school development plan provides an excellent starting point. Part of the school development planning process is to designate a series of development projects for the next academic year. The plan establishes the management priorities. In the responsibility-driven model some individuals would have significantly large task loads for the following year, whereas others may have no specific projects at all, their roles having more of a maintenance focus. A heterarchical approach would see the school development plan as the basis for organizing the management structure for the following year. Project teams could then be set up to manage the projects. By this method management responsibilities would be for specific management tasks and for active membership of temporary task teams. Once a project is completed the team disbands.

Some tasks in a typical school development plan may be quite short-lived, perhaps occupying a small task team for a week or two. Others may be more substantial, ranging over a whole academic year and involving some change of team membership as the project develops. Through the regular pattern of staff meetings, teams refer to the staff as a whole, making periodic reports and receive recommendations, observations, responses and suggestions.

---

*Box 7.4*

*Project team management*

Within the projects teams, status differentials can be minimized, and each member of staff encouraged to contribute according to their experience and skill. There are many benefits to be accrued from such a dynamic and highly participative structure:

- It maximizes staff expertise and experience.
- It involves all staff in key management and leadership activities.
- It achieves a higher work rate.
- It removed the frustrations often experienced when decision-making is attempted in too large a group.
- It develops new skills and expertise.
- It facilitates professional development.
- It increases enjoyment and commitment.
- It makes better use of time.
- It allows quicker responses to new problems.

---

Perhaps more than anything this sort of approach to shared leadership helps a school to move from a red light mentality, i.e. restricting access to action and development, to a green light mentality, i.e. encouraging easy access and involvement in the key tasks of school development. Devolving authority to the task and its team will release heads from too detailed an involvement in development and change, and allow the fuller expression of staff talent and ambition. Teams should be encouraged to set their own detailed targets within the brief designed by the staff as a whole.

In practice a combination of these two approaches is desirable, with individuals carrying some responsibility for receiving information and keeping it flowing, noting developments and identifying projects. When tasks are needed, such as the production of draft policy documents, curriculum plans or reports to governors, these are best tackled in small teams where the process of collaboration reduces isolation, increases motivation and enables work to be completed more effectively and within shorter deadlines.

---

In this section a heterarchical approach to school management has been outlined. Reflect on the management structure of your own school, and your role within it, and consider the extent to which:

- Project and task teams are a dynamic feature of school life.
- Job descriptions assume individual and separate responsibilities.
- The project team approach poses challenges as well as solutions.

---

## Collaboration

In the context of rapid and accelerating change it may no longer be possible to rely on separation and individualism to run effective organizations. Survival and effectiveness depend upon those working in organizations to discover and develop more efficient and effective ways of satisfying the numerous and varied work demands that are created. A great deal of the stress experienced in organizations comes from the fact that in too many situations members of the same organization seem to be competing with each other rather than collaborating.

The organizational principle of schooling is individualism – the single teacher and the class has become established as the fundamental work unit in schools. The curriculum is built around this notion, the timetable organizes it and work is allocated on the basis of it. The notion has extended into the management of schools so that individuals have been encouraged to accept and undertake management tasks different from those of their colleagues. The process of moving from individualism to collaboration is difficult and sometimes painful.

---

*Box 7.5*
*More than the sum of the parts*
Ray Krok (1977) has coined the phrase

None of us is as good as all of us

to underline the enormous potential lying untapped and unused in most organizations, potential that can only be released by bringing individuals together in powerful work alliances, often temporary ones, to tackle the unending flow of tasks, projects and demands that arrive daily in most schools.

---

Stress is a sign that current structures are incapable of meeting new demands and constantly changing situations. Collaboration has the capability to enable most organizations to increase both their efficiency and their effectiveness.

In order to bring about a significant shift from individualism to collaboration, notions of leadership need to be rethought and new definitions agreed. Leadership can no longer continue only to be associated with the roles and responsibilities of senior members of management teams. The whole staff needs to be seen as the management team, and leadership as the set of skills and qualities that can emerge at any level to move things forward. A suggestion, an initiative or a small but significant action can each be regarded as leadership if it moves tasks forward, supports the activities of others and enables aims and intentions to be achieved.

In a whole range of organizations, management structures and processes are changing to meet new and uncertain situations. Schools as organizations will need to develop an altogether new style of flexibility. A style that is task driven rather than built around lasting responsibilities.

## Developing a team approach

Professional work in schools has developed from a tradition of separateness – teachers working alone with groups of learners in classrooms. This plays a significant part in our career choice, allowing optimum conditions for personal autonomy and individual expression. We like the freedom to determine our own ways of working and take our own decisions. Our skills and capabilities have been built on this individualistic assumption. If we had wanted a job where the key features were collaboration and teamwork we may have opted for a different sort of career. Consequently, teachers do not always find the collaborative modes demanded by current pressures an easy option.

The vital priority for schools over the next few years is to question every assumption on which their management and leadership has been built, and to ask the question: what will be the costs of clinging on to the assumptions and principles we have brought with us from the past?

This will involve building and developing a management culture designed to serve and satisfy the human spirit, rather than one designed to keep people in their place, to keep them to task and to make them painfully aware of their deficiencies.

The team approach to management is a very challenging option and it will demand that we start from small beginnings and build gradually. Experimenting with teams of two is likely to show the value of collaboration and introduce a new spirit of co-operation and collegiality. It will be necessary to break down distinctions between innovation and development. People will have to learn as they carry out new challenges, not in order to carry them out. Few in the organization will ever have the skills for the next innovation, and these will need to be acquired quickly, as the change is introduced. These changed conditions will require new structures for school INSET days, and demand a new emphasis to professional development planning. The notion of the learning organization has been with us for some time. It underlines the idea that no organization in conditions of fast change can ever be fully prepared for new challenges. What will single out the successful organizations from the weaker ones is their capacity to learn fast and to adapt.

---

*Box 7.6*
*The precious resource*
(Hampden-Turner, 1990)
What is really scarce and precious is a corporate culture of people who have learnt to work sensitively together. That cannot be stolen, cannot be appropriated. No one can imitate it. It is unique. The people who can do that are the most precious and vital resource for any organization.

---

The inevitable move towards collaboration does not mean that all work must be carried out in teams, groups or partnerships. A proper individualism is vital to the successful management of work and the effective use of human resources. What it does mean, is a greater capacity to think collectively and utilize the skills and qualities of people in more creative and effective ways.

- What is your own experience of teamwork, either in sport, in social activity or at work?
- To what extent do you value the tradition of individuality and autonomy in teaching? What challenges does a staff of individualists pose to those in senior management?
- What is your view of the structural changes that will be necessary if school management is to come through the evolutionary challenge successfully?

# Building effective teams

Organizations that succeed in using team development as a key part of their management structure are the ones best poised to:

- make leaps in innovation
- improve quality
- increase efficiency
- improve performance.

Some of the issues that need to be considered in moving to team development are:

- *Relationship of teams to the school decision-making process* To harness the potential of an organization it is vital to bring as many participants as possible into the co-management process and to give them an active share in creating vision and policy, designing strategy, making decisions and evaluating effectiveness. Commitment to organizational aims and aspirations can only be achieved where there is a close connection of individuals to the determining of policies and plans.
- *The nature of authority invested in teams* Teams need to be given real power and authority to manage tasks and projects. They need to be able to work without constant referral to senior managers, and encouraged to determine their own priorities, decide working methods and make appropriate decisions.
- *Ground rules for team management* Within an overall plan for team management, individual teams need opportunity and scope to experiment, to learn and to develop effective working practices. This means access to training in team development. There is no one way to run an effective management team, and flexibility, creativity and imagination need to be high priorities. It is important not to invest too high an expectation in team management too soon. Teams need to build confidence and develop skill through achievement and suc-

cess. In the early stages of team management, tasks need to be clear, of short duration and within the capacity of the team to deliver. Success can be the most effective building block.

John Nicholson (1992) has produced a useful set of distinctions between a group and a team (Figure 7.2).

| Group | Team |
|-------|------|
| Individuals work independently | Time is not wasted struggling over territory |
| Members act like hired hands | Members feel ownership for their unit |
| Suggestions are not encouraged | Members apply unique talents to team objectives |
| Members distrust colleagues because they do not understand their roles | Members can express ideas and opinions |
| Disagreement is seen as divisive | Disagreement is acceptable |
| Members are cautious about what they say | Members try to understand one another's point of view |
| Members don't know how to resolve conflicts | Conflict is seen as an opportunity for new ideas and creativity |
| Members believe it's more important to do as others do than to produce positive results | Members participate in decisions aimed at achieving positive results |

*Figure 7.2* Differences between groups and teams

Research into the conduct and management of teams in organizations has accumulated evidence about the characteristics that typify effectiveness and ineffectiveness. There is no magic formula for the creation of successful teams. Each of the characteristics listed in the team column can only be brought about by the individual team members deciding to behave in a particular way. In a team each of the participants is responsible for their own behaviour, the nature and style of their contributions, the quality of support they offer to team colleagues and the way they make their own knowledge, skills and qualities available to the team.

In a climate of management uncertainty, with new and unexpected tasks arriving increasingly regularly, it makes no sense to tie people to fixed and inflexible roles. Management structures need a new quality of adhocracy – the capacity to respond to new tasks quickly and efficiently. Fixed role management can create severe difficulties for modern organizations:

● It can create an imbalance in work. Some individuals can find themselves hugely overloaded while others remain temporarily free of any major tasks.

- Time allocations for changes are shorter than they were. Innovations have to be put in place much quicker.
- Many of the tasks are such that previous experience is not guaranteed to help. There is a novelty to many innovations for which no ready expertise may exist.

Management activity needs to be less concerned with defining areas of responsibility and more concerned with what needs doing next. Senior managers in schools have found themselves disproportionately challenged by change because of the novelty of new tasks and challenges. Staff already have full and extensive portfolios of responsibility so that senior staff seem to have no choice but to take on more themselves. What is required is a new concept, a new way of managing fast change and complexity.

In most schools today, in virtually all responsibility areas, there is more work than individuals can ever hope to accomplish. A great deal of management ingenuity will be required if this trend is to be challenged.

---

*Box 7.7*

*The back-burner*

One of the most useful concepts in the management of heavy pressure and demand is the notion of the *back-burner* – where material can be kept at a low rate of combustion until it needs to be brought forward for more urgent attention.

Schools will have to be tougher about priorities. This will involve deciding not to do some things at all, and deciding to carry out others to a more moderate level of achievement. The key decision will be about which tasks the school will really want to do well. A new ruthlessness about priorities will require courage and sensitive leadership. The new proverb – if a job is not worth doing well it is not worth doing at all – will become increasingly significant.

By using the concept of the back-burner we place things in a queue according to their priority and in relation to the resources available to deal with them.

---

Using the back-burner does not mean that we reject tasks or opt out of responsibilities, it means that we place tasks and projects in an appropriate framework of priority according to importance, feasibility and resources available. We must stop believing we can, and should, try and do everything at once. Effective management is the art of painful choice.

By using the school development plan as the driving force of management and leadership we focus energy where it really counts – on those activities where there is a declared intention to bring about specific outcomes and achievements. Strategic work consists of different types of management activity and the design and staffing of teams needs to reflect this.

---

*Box 7.8*
*Types of team*
Different types of team will be required:

- envisioning teams
- forecasting teams
- task interpretation teams
- design teams
- planning teams
- start-up teams
- organizing teams
- development teams
- completer teams
- review teams
- research teams
- feedback teams
- training teams
- enquiry teams
- brainstorming teams
- problem-solving teams.

---

It is useful to appreciate that major strategic projects, such as significant curriculum change, consist of a sequence of phases. Staff expertise can sometimes be optimized by establishing different staff combinations for the different phases. When we work on our own, handling each of the phases by ourselves, we become very aware that we have a pattern of strengths and weaknesses. Some of us are really good at planning, others at devising practical methodologies and others at tying up loose ends. The team approach gives us the opportunity to build alliances of expertise, increasing the likelihood of high-quality results. Teams can also serve a vital professional development purpose when we work with more able and skilful colleagues, learning from them and improving our own qualities and capabilities.

While it is important that management structure reflects the declared intentions and policies contained in the school development plan, a number of unexpected projects and tasks are likely to arise in the course of the school year. These can be dealt with by *ad hoc* or standby teams, perhaps consisting of those who are not currently involved in the team structure.

At the heart of task group effectiveness will be the quality of team communication and the ways in which individuals can exercise their interpersonal skills and qualities in the collaborative setting.

> ● Reflect on the differences between groups and teams. How are the different characteristics demonstrated in the collaborative ventures in your school?
> ● How could you apply the concept of the back-burner in your role?
> ● What different types of team would suit your staff (Box 7.7)?

## Team management

Successful teams are created when skilful people come together and are able through the process of sharing and collaboration to release their skills and qualities to achieve consistently high-quality results. The process of successful collaboration has a number of key elements (Figure 7.3).

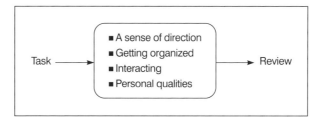

*Figure 7.3* The collaborative process

### Task

Without a task there can be little purpose. In addition to simply stating the job of work that needs to be done, a well-phrased task statement sets out a professional challenge. The team can choose to aim high, and give the task their best effort, or take a minimalist approach and decide merely to satisfy declared or perceived expectations. Teams which aim low tend to have little self-respect, their members are unlikely to be challenged by team membership and are unlikely to derive personal and professional satisfaction from working together. For the enterprising and high aiming team, tasks are accepted as voyages of discovery, invitations into the unknown and opportunities for breaking new ground.

### A sense of direction

Good teams know where they are going. They spend time sorting out intentions and clarifying purposes and end results. They work hard to create in the mind of each team member a strong visual image of what they want to achieve. This not only reinforces intention, it minimizes the possibility of ending up with something that nobody wanted.

### Getting organized

This involves constant attention to process and procedure. Experimenting and refining systematic frameworks, and modifying rules and procedures all combine to increase efficiency through shared understanding. Awareness of the time element means that expectations are set realistically, within the resources available.

Above all, getting organized means harnessing and activating the collaborative capabilities present within the team:

- understanding – knowing what to do
- skill – being able to do it
- commitment – wanting to do it
- success – being capable of achieving it.

### Interacting

Good teams are those where team members demonstrate communication skills at a high level. Among the interpersonal skills of special importance in teamwork are:

- thinking
- listening
- handling ideas
- supporting other team members
- providing encouragement
- sharing feelings
- offering feedback
- voicing worries and concerns
- declaring difficulties
- making decisions
- generating energy
- building commitment
- self-discipline – resisting the temptation to take up air time without a really good reason
- celebrating achievement.

## Personal qualities

These involve behaving in ways that are comfortable with oth
colleagues – being open and honest, speaking directly, appreciating the
efforts of others and being aware that effective behaviour is a matter of
choice not accident.

## Review

Improving the quality of teamwork involves a commitment to learning
through experience. Reviewing is the process of submitting experience
to analysis in order to understand the processes of collaboration,
building on successful practice and eliminating the ineffective and
unsuccessful.

---

Box 7.9
Developing effective teamwork
The following agenda for process development provides a useful
checklist for review:

- How can we develop awareness and understanding of the
workings of the team and the nature of the contributions made
by individuals and groups?
- How can we foster and facilitate effective relationships between
colleagues?
- How can we enhance the quality of communications?
- How can we define and develop roles, tasks and methods of
evaluation?
- How can we assess member well-being and locate personal
causes of difficulty?
- How can we promote and increase flexibility and
connectedness?
- How can we create a climate of permanent change and
preparedness for initiative?
- How can we motivate and enable each other to suggest
changes?
- How can we support each other in the process of implementing
change?
- How can we work together to create the conditions in which
everyone can give of their best consistently?

---

# Meetings

Much management teamwork is conducted in the form of meetings
and these have not tended to be popular with teachers.

x 7.10

*ıe trouble with meetings*

,eetings are often an unpopular form of doing business owing to:

- overloaded agendas
- vague agendas or no agendas at all
- excessive time is spent on issues to do with previous meetings – minutes, matters arising etc.
- lack of information about agenda items, decisions to be made, issues to be discussed
- poor attention to circumstances – location, timing, seating, refreshments etc.
- domination of discussion by few participants
- lack of structure to the meeting
- bad timing of items
- failure to involve all participants
- slavish attention to traditional procedures – 'through you, chair', proposers and seconders, formal terminology
- confusion about purposes
- inability to attend to the feelings of participants
- lack of leadership
- failure to honour time agreements
- inability to handle disagreements creatively and openly.

If teamwork is to succeed in schools then new and effective ways of handling meetings need to be developed. It is useful to consider the management of meetings as having four distinct phases:

- planning and preparation
- conducting the meeting
- reviewing the meeting
- follow-up.

### Planning and preparation

Among the issues to be dealt with are:

- place, date and time
- facilities, resources, refreshments
- notification to all those involved
- documentation – minutes, agendas, reports
- the organization and management of the meeting – order of items, purposes and end results for meeting as a whole and for each item, and roles and responsibilities.

In large organizations it is useful to have a ways and means group that will manage the overall strategy for meetings. The planning for individual meetings is best left to the individuals and groups most closely involved in the specific agenda items.

## Conducting the meeting

Different agenda items need different approaches and different forms of leadership. In these days of complex agendas it makes little sense to have one person chairing or leading a whole meeting. Items need to fit into an overall time plan and then be managed by the individual or group most closely connected with it. Among the important tasks for whole meetings and separate agenda items are

- introduction and briefing
- clarifying purposes and intended end results
- outlining methods and procedures to be used
- agreeing management roles – timekeeper, chair, notetaker or charting scribe.

The more people who are involved in the management of teamwork, the faster leadership experience grows, and with it a deeper understanding of the complex processes involved. Among the leadership issues that will need attention are:

- gaining agreement about appropriate methods and techniques to get all participants involved
- dealing with individuals
- summarizing progress
- handling disagreements and misunderstandings
- recording decisions
- moving things on
- attending to process – how the meeting is progressing, how people are feeling and time management.

## Reviewing the meeting

It is surprising how little this features in the management of meetings in most organizations. Far too often people come away from meetings grumbling about its bad management, the behaviour of a selfish few and the reflection that it was a complete waste of time. No organization these days can afford to have any participant feeling that they are wasting their time. The energy created through bad experience of meetings needs to be transformed so that all dissatisfactions become vital issues for attention.

Process needs to be a deliberate and constant agenda item, so that people feel that the costly coming together of staff is properly recognized in the quality of preparation and planning that goes into meetings. Providing time to review the experience of a meeting is the sure way to bring about improvement, increase interest and commitment and generate greater efficiency and effectiveness.

No meeting should ever finish without a review into its management being conducted by all those taking part. At its simplest this can be a few minutes sharing the successes and difficulties of the meeting and making suggestions about how things can be improved in the future. It is essential that those responsible for preparing and managing meetings take note of these reviews and act on the suggestions that are made. This perhaps more than anything else helps to create a sense of shared endeavour and co-management, increasing commitment all round.

### Follow-up

This involves making sure that decisions made in meetings are acted upon. Originally, minutes were distributed to participants the day after a meeting as a reminder of decisions made and actions required. Nowadays, the practice seems to be that you receive minutes with your agenda for the next meeting, when it is far too late to act on a decision made. Among the important management tasks of follow-up to meetings are:

- distributing action summaries to all concerned
- arranging for those who were absent to be informed
- noting key review recommendations and passing them on
- arranging for flipcharts to be displayed or typed up and distributed.

## Teamwork methods and techniques

### Break with tradition

Far too many meetings in schools display the characteristics that were the subject of company legislation laid down in the nineteenth century – formal chairing, rigid agendas, minutes, matters arising, any other business, the dominance of the plenary format and the reliance on open discussion.

Given the complexity of the demands affecting modern management, it is vital to break away from the inhibiting structures of this tradition and develop more imaginative and creative ways of making decisions, solving problems, developing policy and managing strategy. The following methods and techniques have all been used to this purpose in a range of organizations.

## Clarify intentions

No meeting should ever start, or even be convened, unless all participants are clear about the purposes and intended end results. An effective way to ensure this is to check that everyone has similar responses to two sentence stems:

- We are holding this meeting in order to . . .
- What we will end up with is . . .

The first of these helps to clarify purposes for the meeting – 'We are holding this meeting in order to:
1 Clarify roles and responsibilities for the term.
2 Fix dates for end of term activities.
3 Decide on representation on staff committees.'

The second helps all participants to create a clear mental picture of what the tangible outcomes will be – 'What we will end up with is:
1 Details of post holders and their specific responsibilities and action targets.
2 Dates in diaries for end of term activities.
3 A list of staff representatives.'

Clarifying these right at the beginning of a meeting enables participants to embark on the agenda with clarity of purpose, and a clear idea of what needs to be achieved.

## Create a process structure

Far too often the agenda – a list of items to be dealt with – acts as the plan for the meeting. What is needed is a more fundamental plan that provides all the information necessary to enable participants to share in its co-management. Elements of the plan will be:

- place, time, venue
- purposes and end results – the meeting as whole and for each separate item
- the overall time allocation for the meeting and for each of the agenda items, including the review
- who will be managing the various parts of the meeting and specific roles and responsibilities
- the methods and techniques to be employed for each item.

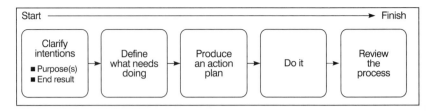

*Figure 7.4* A framework for meetings

Figure 7.4 shows one possible structure. This framework can be used to:

- plan whole meetings
- plan specific agenda items
- guide the process of a meeting
- focus energy
- separate preparation and planning from action
- develop efficiency and effectiveness.

It is useful to display this structure on a whiteboard or flipchart, making it a useful focal point for the meeting.

### Personal reflection

The only thinking time most participants have in meetings is while someone else is talking. Most meetings are noisy, characterized by one verbal contribution after another. This means that most participants are operating in spontaneous mode all the time, talking off the top of their heads. The thinking and consideration that does go on has to be managed at the expense of not listening carefully to other participant's contributions. This is extremely inefficient, and potentially damaging to the quality of decisions made.

One way to increase the quality of individual contributions and enable all participants to gather and then offer their thoughts and ideas is to create personal reflection time. Two or three minutes of silence at strategic moments when people think and jot down responses to a question, list possible courses of action or note potential costs and benefits can fundamentally change the dynamics of a meeting, making it more thoughtful, participative and effective. After the moments of silence it is useful to go round and take each persons contribution in turn. This has a number of benefits. It removes the sense of competition that attends many meetings – fighting to get your ideas in before someone else. It makes sure that all contributions have been thought about first, and it enables all people to contribute. Above all it improves the quality of listening – all participants have thought about their contribution, know they will have their turn to express it, and know that it will be received respectfully by the other members.

Teams which employ personal reflection often find they can conduct business much more quickly, experiencing a greater sense of participation and a greatly increased sense of satisfaction.

## Brainstorming

One of the tendencies in predominantly discursive meetings is towards negation. An idea is put forward and others look for and express faults with it. Such a negative process tends to inhibit creativity and make people cautious about expressing ideas and opinions. Brainstorming is a device designed to inhibit this negative inclination. Its purpose is to create as many ideas as possible in a short space of time – four or five minutes. It is essential that the rules are upheld – that there shall be no challenging or contradicting of contributions, that all ideas are admissible and that contributions are recorded, preferably on a whiteboard or flipchart where all can see them. Brainstorming is an excellent way to create energy, get an agenda item going, involve all participants and generate a range of options to choose from.

## Index cards/Post-its

Another highly effective way of generating options, ideas and possibilities in a short space of time is to start with a few minutes of personal reflection time and ask people to record their ideas on index cards. These can then be collected in, laid out and sorted into categories which can then be worked on. Using this method it is often possible to make more progress in ten minutes than discussion meetings achieve in an hour. Post-its are a useful alternative – they can be stuck to a wall and moved from place to place.

A further benefit of this method is that ideas are permanently recorded in an efficient way – they are ready-made minutes, can be stored and retrieved easily and can be split up and used by different groups.

## Recording progress

Effective teams tend to make their creativity visible. They record their thinking where it can be seen – on a whiteboard or flipchart. It is tragic how many good ideas get lost in meetings because they go unrecorded or only noted on individual jotters. The visual focus created by clearly visible lists can help to increase creativity and the making of connections between different ideas. Flipcharts can also be permanent records and ongoing thinking sheets – available after meetings for further ideas and contributions.

## Subgroups

Once the membership of a meeting goes above six or seven it can become inefficient to run it in plenary format. As size increases so the contribution time per member decreases. Also as size increases the tendency for people to feel comfortable expressing thoughts, feelings and ideas decreases. These difficulties can be overcome by subdividing into groups from time to time – sometimes only for a minute or two. Following a few minutes of personal reflection it can be highly effective to break the team into pairs to talk through their jottings. This further helps the process of personal clarification, gives ideas a gentle airing before they are offered to the whole group and ensures the optimum of participation.

Running some agenda items as subgroup tasks can also be effective. In this way it is possible to increase the workload of a meeting without requiring greater effort from the participants.

### Timing

The importance of good timekeeping has already been stressed. The plan needs to have allocated chunks of time to each agenda item. In order to be efficient it is necessary to keep to time. It is very helpful for one of the participants to monitor the time – offering gentle reminders about progress and the amount of time left. The presence of a large-faced clock or an electronic timer can also help people to be time conscious and play their part in efficient management of the meeting.

While it is vital to manage time well, it is also important not to be inflexible. Time allocations are often misjudged, and it may be necessary to adjust schedules, sometimes agreeing to abandon less vital items until a future occasion. It is important to try to keep within the overall time limit set for a meeting. Always adding time on to the end of meetings encourages slackness and inefficiency – it is usually a sign of bad team leadership.

### Leadership

Leadership in meetings is invariably associated with the role of chairing. More flexible and less separated forms of leadership in teams need to be developed. It is important to establish the idea that leadership is not simply the behaviour of a person in charge, but those behaviours which move the team forward, create good ideas and enable good decisions to be made. In this sense leadership can merge from any member of the team. Some of the best management teams eschew formal leadership, letting circumstances, interests and expediency determine team roles and responsibilities.

Formal leadership in meetings can be useful in holding the process together and keeping the meeting on course. It is important to break away from the traditional concepts that have attended the chairing role. These have placed the definition of the role firmly in the hands of the chairperson who runs the meeting according to personal whim.

Team authority then becomes detached from the team. A more enterprising approach is for the team itself to determine the role and function of the chair and to give authority to any of the team who agree to take it on. The role then serves the purposes of the team and all team members can take their turn as appropriate.

- Consider the questions in Box 7.8. What specific practical strategies could you initiate to help develop more effective teamwork?
- What is your experience of meetings? Create your own checklist of bad experiences, but also note what has happened when you have really enjoyed being part of a meeting.
- Consider the methods and techniques outlined in the final section of the chapter. How could you incorporate some of these in your work?

# 8 The learning school

The illiterate of the future will no longer be the individual who cannot read. It will be the person who does not know how to learn how to learn.
(Toffler, 1971)

## Introduction

One of the most significant challenges facing those responsible for the future direction of the schooling system in this country is the conceptual relationship between learning and teaching. Learning has been seen as the product of teaching – a passive process of receiving and assimilating. We need to develop a new understanding of this relationship in which learning is the active and dynamic force at work, and teaching is the means by which the appropriate support and guidance for that process can be provided. Schools will have a vital part to play in this shift of understanding, not only to benefit future generations of pupils but to enable themselves to adapt and survive in a turbulent and continuously changing world.

This chapter will:

- examine assumptions about learning and how we will need to develop them
- explore the characteristics and features of a learning organization
- consider the need for schools to introduce a research and development facility
- discuss the dynamics of the change process
- outline ways in which professional learning will need to develop in the future.

## The evolutionary challenge

As we move into a new century and a new millennium we face both the dilemmas of the present and the challenges of the future. Perhaps for the first time in our history we cannot be sure that what we provide for pupils in schools today will equip them as the adults of tomorrow, to face a turbulent and fast-changing world with capability and confidence.

> Box 8.1
> *The possibility of extinction*
> (Macy, 1995)
> Until the late twentieth century, every generation throughout history lived with the tacit certainty that there would be generations to follow. Each assumed, without questioning, that its children and children's children would walk the same earth, under the same sky. Hardships, failures, and personal death were encompassed in that vaster assurance of continuity. That certainty is now lost to us, whatever our politics. That loss, unmeasured and immeasurable, is the pivotal psychological reality of our time.

In our societies and their institutions we have not yet learnt to be comfortable in this increasingly troubled, turbulent and confusing world, and we tend to react with panic to situations that seem to take us unawares. Much of the recent legislation affecting education has had this panic element about it, and adaptive measures have been taken without sufficient attention to the deep lying problems of an education system in a fast-changing world. It is almost as if a terrible concern to keep up appearances has overwhelmed us, whatever the consequences.

This tendency of governments to ignore the wider issues and longer-term implications of education, and to concentrate only on panic measures, creates a vacuum in the management of schools. The education community and the schools themselves have found their creativity crushed in the grip of heavily centralized direction. And so it is to the schools themselves, and the wider education community, that we must now look to provide a new wave of creative innovation that will take us into the next century. This will require vision rather than dogma, and imagination rather than regulation.

The agenda for this adaptive innovation will be considerable. Five particular considerations are crucial:

- participation in learning
- the concept of delivery
- education for living
- inner worlds
- leadership into the future.

### Participation in learning

Among the many assumptions about education that will need to change, is the idea that schools are concerned only with the learning of their pupils. The complex and continuously changing demands of the future will require that staff and pupils see themselves as co-learners, working together to ensure that the school takes account of change, and uses all its combined insights and understandings to support the evolutionary adaptations required. Schools must change from places predominantly concerned with teaching, to institutions of learning. Adaptation and survival require that we become adept at understanding the turbulence of the environment and responding to it with imagination and creativity.

Learning is a natural process and one of the most powerful forces in our lives. We have become used in recent years to references to *steep learning curves* as we find ourselves challenged by new roles, changed circumstances and novel situations. Learning is the means by which, at any stage of our lives, we adapt in a world characterized by complexity and turbulence. Schools must become places dedicated to the phenomenon of the *learning curve*.

## The concept of delivery

We have inherited the idea that schools are institutions of delivery – handing on traditional orthodoxy and received wisdom to the next generation. Schools will increasingly need to see themselves as organizations of acquisition – seeking to gather knowledge, experience and insight in the interests of school development and to serve the needs of its community. Pupils themselves will become creators of databases that other pupils will use in their studies, and co-educators alongside their teachers. Perhaps we have to realize that we are all educators now, in powerful learning and teaching relationships with each other. The many and varied skills existing within the immediate community of any school will need to be harnessed as a resource for the whole community and channelled through the school.

We must move beyond the assumption that the school curriculum is something devised by the adult generation for delivery to the unsuspecting young. The young themselves need a role in determining the means by which they prepare for their own future, and we must drop the arrogant belief that they are incapable of such an involvement. The curriculum needs to be seen as theirs, not as a legal requirement of them by their elders. It is both sad and tragic that among the plethora of National Curriculum documents circulated to schools, governors and parents, not one has been produced to explain its purposes and process to the children themselves, who are supposed to be its beneficiaries.

This shift in assumptions will involve a change from seeing schooling as a legal requirement, to the idea of learning as a right and an entitlement.

## Education for living

As the disintegration and fragmentation of our traditional social institutions continues, the pupils in our schools will demand a curriculum for learning that addresses the changed and changing circumstances of their world. The children now in our schools will be the first generation to live all of their lives as both national participants and global citizens. Traditional curriculum content gives scant attention to the knowledge and skills required to live fully in this more interdependent world.

The current imperatives of enculturation, and preparation for the world of work, will be insufficient to develop the skills and capabilities needed in the future. Increasingly important will be a curriculum that focuses on learning for living, that attends to the developmental processes so important in helping children to search for meaning in their lives, to develop deep and enriching relationships and to communicate with skill across the diminishing boundaries that once separated the different national groups across the world.

This will involve a shift more significant than any we have made in recent years. As adults and teachers we must appreciate that we may not actually know what is best for our children, some of whom will live into the twenty-second century. We must come down from our arrogant pedestal where we see it as our right to prepare children for the world that we have made, and realize that we have a responsibility to educate them for the one that they themselves will create.

## Inner worlds

Central to this significant transformation towards education for life and living will be a major shift from an obsession with the outer world of appearance, behaviour and performance, to a proper concern for the inner world of moods, reflections, fantasies, feelings, images, thoughts, fears, frustrations, hopes and dreams. We have inherited a belief that giving attention to the inner world of children is inappropriate, indeed some believe that children are empty vessels and that it is our duty to fill them up as soon as possible. It is the rejection of any significance to the inner world of children that has contributed to the alienating dynamics of the generation gap. Developing a more sensitive attention to how children think and feel about their lives is one of the major challenges in the development of the schooling system. It means that we must stop seeing education as a means of managing the lives of the young, and begin to see it as a process of leadership – helping children to equip themselves for the long and challenging journey into a future that we cannot predict for them.

## Leadership into the future

The idea that people do not want to be managed, but want to be led, captures the essence of the evolutionary challenge for schools. It is a challenge that schools had, in fact, taken up over thirty years ago through school-based initiatives, and through the innovative and pioneering projects of the Schools Council. It is almost as if the obsession with external control through educational legislation interrupted a vital process of change that was already well under way in our schools. It is sobering to speculate just how far our schools would have progressed if they had not been interrupted and hindered in their own process of adaptation and change. What the system now needs is passionate, caring and imaginative leadership in schools, leadership which activates and empowers the naturally present potentialities for learning of all children.

For those managing schools during the transitional years into the next millennium the task is considerable. It will involve new thinking and new ways of handling both existing and emerging challenges. While the strategic functions of management will continue to be crucial, it will be the processes of leadership, guidance and support that will become the key to effective change and development, creating schools which are as concerned with hope as they have been with behaviour, with enterprise as they have been with intelligence and with imagination as they have been with objectivity.

| Old paradigm assumptions | New paradigm assumptions |
|---|---|
| ■ Emphasis on content, acquiring a body of 'right' information, once and for all. | ■ Emphasis on learning how to learn. |
| ■ Learning as a product, a destination. | ■ Learning as a process, a journey. |
| ■ Hierarchical and authoritarian structure, rewarding conformity and punishing dissent. | ■ Pupils and teachers see each other as partners and not as roles. |
| ■ Relatively rigid structure, prescribed curriculum. | ■ Flexible structures, varied starting points, mixed learning experiences. |
| ■ Age-related learning. | ■ Integration of age groupings. Learning not age specific. |
| ■ Priority on performance. | ■ Priority given to the self-concept as the key determinant of successful learning. |
| ■ Emphasis on external world. Inner experience considered inappropriate in school setting. | ■ Use of pupil's inner experience as context for learning. |
| ■ Guessing and divergent thinking discouraged. | ■ Guessing and divergent thinking encouraged as part of the creative learning process. |
| ■ Emphasis on analytical, left-brain thinking. | ■ More emphasis on right-brain, intuitive activity. |
| ■ Classroom designed for efficiency and convenience. | ■ More concern for the learning environment – colour, comfort, personal space and privacy. |
| ■ Education seen as an age-related social necessity. | ■ Education as a lifelong process only partially related to schools. |
| ■ Teacher as instructor and imparter of knowledge. | ■ Teacher as learner too, learning from the pupils. |

*Figure 8.1* The paradigm shift in learning

The shift required to bring about a conceptual, and eventually practical change, in our approach to the management of learning has been outlined by Marylin Ferguson (1982) and is set out in Figure 8.1.

A *business as usual* approach will not do. Perhaps for the first time in our history we will need to look to our own learning first. In the future, arrival in a management role will not imply acquired expertise, it will indicate that we have demonstrated our capacity to learn at least as fast as the environment around us is changing, and to work powerfully in collaboration with others to empower the processes of adaptation and change.

- Reflect on Joanna Macy's apocalyptic assertion (Box 8.1). How do you react to this view and what implications does it have for your work as an educator?
- Consider each of the five considerations discussed in this section. How far do these relate to your own views about the future and the role of schools in it?

## The learning school

A learning school is one which sees beyond the somewhat limited transactions between teachers and pupils, to the idea that all members of the school are a learning community, committed to finding effective pathways into the future. The concept of the *learning organization* has been growing for some years. In the face of rapid and accelerating change it is increasingly necessary to see learning in the organizational context as well as at the individual level.

*Box 8.2*
*The learning organization*
Bob Garratt (1987) argues that learning has become the key developmental commodity of any organization:

Generating and selling know-how and know-why, the learning of the organization and its people, is becoming the core of any organization which has the chance of surviving in the longer term. We already know a lot about organizational learning processes. When this is added to the new ideas on the generation of vision, the refinement of thinking processes, the development of policy and strategy, the notion of managing as a *holistic* process, and the acquisition of new managerial skills from outside the traditional boundaries, then there is a powerful mix available.

*Figure 8.2* The 4P development chain

Perhaps the main characteristic of a truly learning organization is the way in which it uses the 4P development chain (Figure 8.2).

In a learning school there is:

- a preoccupation with purpose, with the forging of a deep understanding about why we do things. A strong sense of purpose is a prerequisite for any worthwhile activity
- a determination to articulate clear, ambitious but realistic policies that declare intentions and which make firm commitments to action
- a deep curiosity about practice with no methodology or technique being taken for granted. Teachers and pupils alike are constantly questioning the means by which the learning process is conducted and striving to gain insights and understandings about its elusive complexities
- a driving ambition about ends and about the nature and quality of the success and achievements of all. The outcomes of learning are seen not only as ends in themselves, but as significant staging posts in a much longer and more varied adventure.

Learning rather than performance will need to become one of the driving imperatives of leadership and management. Until as teachers we recognize that we have as much to learn as the pupils themselves, we are unlikely to create the conditions for a really significant shift in educational practice. As leaders and managers we must accept it as our duty to do our share of learning too, particularly on behalf of our colleagues, constantly seeking to identify new opportunities for development, fresh growth points, significant trends, outmoded practices and unproductive activities.

A major redefinition of the organizational structure will be necessary. One that moves away from the thrall of hierarchical differentiation and aims to bring everyone – pupils and teachers alike, into the co-management of the school. It will seem heretical to some, to conceive of pupils as co-managers of their school, but this is largely because we have inherited beliefs about their unsuitability and incapacity for such a responsibility. Traditional orthodoxy has significantly underestimated the innate capacities of children to manage the important elements of their own world, as a visit to a good nursery class will demonstrate. We have to build the working principle that pupils and teachers are in a vital partnership of interest and endeavour. This does not mean that there is equality of authority or responsibility, but that each participant in school life is valued as having a contribution to make, both to its daily management and its continuing development.

A learning school is one which has significantly transformed the taxonomy of managerial activity. While such concepts as *organizing*, *monitoring*, *taking charge of*, *being responsible for* and *heading up*, will continue to be the stock in trade of managers' work, there will be new concepts which will need to feature more dynamically in their activities than at present:

● attending to inner worlds
● connecting with pupils and colleagues
● exploring ideas
● envisioning futures
● reflecting on experience
● supporting possibilities
● anticipating outcomes
● scanning the environment
● spotting trends
● celebrating successes
● listening constantly.

Role definitions and job descriptions will need to be reconceived to incorporate these concepts. It will mean giving up the idea that there can ever be a simple management role in a school. We are all in the complexity business now, and the sooner we embrace it the better.

The characteristics of a learning school would include:

● clear purposes understood and shared by all
● a set of negotiated principles and values
● a sharing of ambitions for the future – for each individual and for the school as a whole
● a predisposition to learning in pupils and teachers alike
● participative co-management
● constantly developing information chains
● shared accountability
● quality-minded participants
● a focus on flexibility and adaptability
● innovative and experimental development
● networks and alliances
● unbridled curiosity about the future
● comfort in complexity and confusion
● excitement about tomorrow.

The key emphasis will be on discovery as the driving force behind action. This will mean the end of any notion that there can be secrets about information. Keeping people in the dark has been one of the traditional power devices of managers. Information lies at the heart of capability, and it is the receivers rather than the givers of information who must decide how important it is. This will require new relationships of trust and confidentiality. We are all overloaded with information these days, and part of our capacity to manage in the future will be an increased capability in the handling of data, knowing what to keep and what to discard. Information-sharing and keeping people informed will become one of the most important things a learning school does. It will require a rethinking of traditional timetables to incorporate the necessary school-based teach-ins, seminars and conferences that it will undoubtedly demand.

A fast-changing world cannot be managed with fixed ideas. Rowan Gibson (1997) asserts that the learning school will be one that accepts the inevitability of constantly rethinking, and suggests the following six categories where such rethinking is particularly important.

### Rethinking principles

While we have the power to create the future in our schools we must never cease from asking ourselves what we are creating and why. When we rethink principles we are striving to rediscover sense and meaning in an increasingly uncertain world.

### Rethinking competition

For schools, this means questioning the ever growing tendency to see other schools as rivals, competitors and opponents to be beaten through superior performance and higher location in league tables. The concepts behind the learning school also extend to the idea of a learning community where all schools co-operate as partners and co-developers of pathways into the future. Too much competition draws blood and damages spirit. What is needed is a sharing of ingenuity, a coming together of ambition and determination to create an education system truly worthy of our children.

### Rethinking control and complexity

Traditional orthodoxies in management, devised for a world that is past, need to be reconsidered in the light of ever-increasing complexity. We need new models of shared leadership centred on collective aspiration and transformation. Control must not be used to hinder creativity nor inhibit capability, it must be located in ways that encourage and empower them.

### Rethinking leadership

Leadership needs to be seen as a way of releasing all the potentialities and capabilities that accompany each of us into school every day. I also needs to be seen as a function of all roles in the school, not simply the duty of those with the most senior responsibility.

## Rethinking markets

For schools this means rethinking the whole idea of catchment areas and participants. Technology will continue to revolutionize the means by which we can all learn, and schools will have to consider how they adapt to the increasing power of the Internet to provide powerful and effective learning opportunities to learners of all ages. In the various areas of information technology the young have no fear, they are in control and they will relish any opportunity to manage the process for themselves. Schools will continue to develop a powerful community element, providing learning services to anyone who needs them. Schools and libraries will need to collaborate in providing centres where learning projects can be supported.

## Rethinking the world

Schools, like all other institutions and organizations, need to embrace the vast changes taking place at the global level. As Macy has reminded us, our children are the first generation to be aware that they may not survive the gathering ecological crises that are threatening humanity. As adults we are passing on to the next generation global problems on a scale that no previous generation has experienced. They have to be more capable than we have been in dealing with them.

We have a simple choice, Gibson argues. Either we rethink the future and create it for ourselves, or we wait until we are forced into a rethink, the terms of which have been dictated by others.

> - Reflect on Gibson's six principles about rethinking. How do these relate to your school, and your own role within it?
> - Use the list of characteristics of a learning school to review your own institution.
> - In what ways do you see learning as a wider concept than the way we have traditionally used it?

# Learning together

Perhaps one of the most significant changes in the management of learning in the future will be a breakdown of the traditional distinction between research institutions and teaching organizations. Universities have tended to be concerned with the former and schools with the latter. Traditional approaches to research have placed emphasis on large empirical studies that can take a long time to set up and report on. There has also been a problem for schools in finding systematic, effective and cohesive ways of incorporating the plethora of education research material into their developments. The future will demand that research becomes a means of survival as well as a pursuit of the truth. If the truth takes too long to discover then it may be too late to help us. Quicker response times to research enquiries will be necessary, and questions will need to focus more on the specific and immediate needs of particular schools than many research projects have traditionally been concerned with.

Schools themselves will need to become the agents of their own research, and like most modern businesses have their own research and development facilities. Enquiry will become the driving force of the learning school, and the posing of problems, dilemmas and challenges will be a major concern of managers. In education it is no longer useful to rely solely on a specialized community for research work, and schools themselves will need to become more actively involved in setting up their own small-scale research projects to find answers to the pressing questions of the moment. In doing this they will need to move beyond the objectivity usually demanded by traditional empirical methods, and develop approaches more focused on the perceptions and experiences of those involved in school life. More illuminative approaches will be needed, relying on the collectivity of ideas present in most schools.

One approach to this type of research work is participative enquiry, where the research method seeks to unlock those aspects of human understanding and experience which can help in the development of new theories and practices.

---

Box 8.3
*Love the questions*
Rilke (1975) suggests that nothing less than a love affair with questions and curiosity will enable us to gain the power to learn more effectively.

> Be patient toward all that is unsolved in your heart and try to love the questions themselves like locked rooms and books that are written in a foreign tongue. Do not now seek the answers . . . Live the questions.

---

It will not be definitive answers that need to be sought, but ideas, insights and understandings that take us a little further in the quest. Action research methodologies will also be important in the learning school.

---

Box 8.4
*Action research*
(Elliott, 1981)
In broad terms action research can be described as the study of a social situation with a view to improving the quality of action within it. The aim of action research is to feed practical judgement in concrete situations. Action research is concerned with everyday problems experienced, rather than with *theoretical* problems defined by pure researchers within a discipline of knowledge. The validity of the *theories* it generates depends not so much on *scientific* tests of truth, as on their usefulness in helping people act more intelligently and skilfully. In action research *theories* are not validated independently and applied to practice. They are validated through practice.

---

One of the difficulties of managing schools in a turbulent and changing environment lies in the probability that we have significantly underestimated the complexities of learning and teaching. We have assumed that because these processes are as old as the human race itself, we have sufficiently understood them, and that further study of them is unnecessary. The scientific method, and its preoccupation with objective phenomena has tended to dominate the human and life sciences too. We have been led to believe that research can always provide categoric answers to our questions, and can determine the right ways and wrong ways to educate. We have become reliant on fixtures and rigidities to such an extent that we cannot cope with the idea of a continuum of possibilities. The political debate about education is obsessed with a misdirected dispute between so called *traditional* and *progressive* approaches to the management of learning. Is it not possible that we are grappling here with complexities that defy simple explanation? Perhaps learning is an infinitely more varied and intricate process than we have traditionally supposed. One of the key roles of educators, therefore, is to approach our involvement in the learning process in our classrooms with a sense of wonder and curiosity. Enquiry becomes one of the chief features of our professionalism.

The purpose of school-based research will be to drive the engine of organizational learning. Burning questions and topical issues will help to develop an enquiry focused climate within which new understandings and insights will be made possible. A research dimension will create information pathways in our schools so that ideas and possibilities become spread, considered and tested. These in turn will create other questions, produce new angles and fresh lines of enquiry. For too long in our schools pupils have experienced questions as the means of checking their memorizing capacity, rather than as a powerful tool for enquiry. Perhaps it is now time to encourage children to formulate the questions, both about the complex world they are struggling to understand, and to work with them to devise imaginative and effective ways of satisfying the deep learning needs they identify themselves.

Learning must become an enquiry-driven activity, both for pupils and for teachers. As managers we need to lead by example, sharing with others the difficulties inherent in our demanding roles, and inviting colleagues and pupils into the problem-solving process. Status has no monopoly on wisdom, and it is sometimes the naïve questions that the inexperienced ask that really get us to the heart of an issue.

---

*Box 8.5*
*Real questions*
(John-Paul Sartre)
The main difference between children and philosophers is that children ask real questions.

---

There are some implications for recruitment here. When staff are interviewed for posts in schools, one of the considerations as to their suitability should be what particular lines of professional enquiry they are currently interested in, and what particular research projects they would want to join or initiate.

A central feature of the enquiry-led school is a new approach to the management of *failure*. Traditionally, schools have seen themselves as part of a categoric world in which we are either right or wrong. Schooling has tended to be a relentless pursuit of single correct

---

*Box 8.6*
*Learning through experience*
(Pedler, Burgoyne and Boydell, 1991)
Learning organizations strive to create a climate where failures, accidents and breakdowns are declared openly and learned from so that they can be avoided in the future:

> This means making time for review, whatever the work pressures. It means that the leadership style and culture is about learning from experience and not one of allocating blame and punishment. Managers say things like 'Do your best and if it doesn't work, let's talk about it and find out why.' Planning to collect information, to monitor, review and evaluate new ventures is part of the skill of operating the Learning Company.

---

answers to somewhat closed and straightforward questions, and error avoidance has been seen as one of the virtues of the educated.

In a learning school people do not need to deny their errors and mistakes, or to cover them up. They tend to disclose them honestly, openly and perhaps even joyously because they have led to a breakthrough in learning.

In non-learning organizations, it often feels that is just not possible to talk about mistakes. In such organizations we feel awful about the mistakes we make. It is as if there is a terrible organizational sin in wanting to learn through experience – to do even better the things we do well, and to remedy those things that do not work out as we had hoped.

- What are your views of school as its own research agency?
- How might the processes of participative enquiry and action research be used effectively in your school?
- How does your school deal with failure? How are pupils encouraged to view their mistakes?

## The transforming process

A learning school is one which takes the process of change very seriously. Far from seeing change as an occasional event in the life of the school, it sees change as the key process of the times – the means by which an organization adapts and adjusts itself to new circumstances and fresh situations. The learning school recognizes that while the process of change is a familiar experience to all of us, its dynamics are far from simple and that our understanding of its complexities is far from complete. In managing change, the learning school seeks first to understand what meanings and significances the change will have for the people who will be responsible for managing it. Traditional change management has tended to place the emphasis on the change task, expecting people to rally behind decisions whether they like them or not. This is to place the cart very firmly before the horse. Change is not only the art of the possible, it is also the art of the desirable, deeply affecting all participants involved in its processes.

Most of the changes we are concerned with in schools involve us moving away from known positions out into the unknown. This often means that we have to give up things we are familiar with, and adopt practices we have never tried before, often with a short lead in time and with insufficient opportunity for reflection and preparation. Mostly we can take the changes in our stride and modify our professional practice to new needs and requirements. Sometimes, however, we do not like what we are expected to do but realize that adjustments have to be made. Traditional approaches to change management fail to take sufficient account of the impact that change makes on our lives, and how it affects our capacity to function effectively. It is with this issue that the learning school is concerned.

The process of change involves moving from the known into the unknown (Figure 8.3).

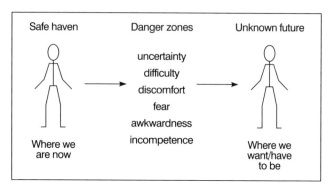

*Figure 8.3* The change process

It is useful to consider change in relation to four aspects of adaptation (Whitaker, 1997):

- *Conceptual change* Changes to the way we think about our work, conceive of our roles and responsibilities, how we assess our effectiveness, how we see the nature of change in our lives and our attitudes to the specific issue of change under consideration.
- *Emotional change* How we feel about the changes proposed, the sorts of challenges and demands it will make on us, the emotions that will be aroused as we begin to struggle with new ideas and fresh expectations, our hopes of success and our fears of failure.
- *Aspirational change* Our hopes and ambitions for our work, our professional mission in life, our commitment to the school and its vision for the future, our career aspirations and our hopes for the sort of contribution we want to make.
- *Practical change* How we stop doing things we have always done and start doing other things we have never done before. How we adapt to new practices and approaches, how we acquire new skills and how we adopt new behaviours.

When we consider going on a journey it is useful to have a map of the route. It is not enough to be told where we should go, and that we have a certain amount of time to get there. We need help with three vital questions:

- What is the purpose of the journey?
- What will the journey be like?
- What will we do when we get there?

Here we have yet another use for the 4P development chain. This can help us to focus on different aspects of a proposed change, and help those who will be involved to make the journey in ways which reduce confusion and distress and which provide stepping stones into the future.

In considering these key issues we need to appreciate that change is as much an inner process of adjustment as a practical task. How we feel about what we are expected to do significantly affects how we do it. We need to realize that resistance to change is one way that people register, without actually saying so directly, that they are uncomfortable, perhaps afraid of what is proposed. Good managers never assume that anyone finds change easy or even acceptable. Expressing our concerns about changes which profoundly affect us is natural, and should be expected. Time needs to be allocated for these concerns, so that they can be dealt with sensitively and openly.

Traditionally, we have approached change in a somewhat clumsy manner, defining the tasks that need to be accomplished and driving people on. There are more effective ways, ones that respect natural human concerns and misgivings. A preoccupation with ends often involves only cursory attention to the means by which those ends will be achieved, yet it is the means which can be so fearful. We must never forget Marshall McLuhan's prophetic epithet – *the medium is the message*. The change journey is illustrated in Figure 8.4.

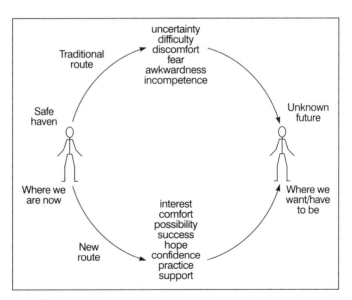

*Figure 8.4* The change journey

The behaviour of managers in the change process is crucial. Impatience to get things moving tends to indicate an undue preoccupation with the task and a lack of concern with those who will be responsible for implementing it. Proper attention to the process itself will tend to communicate itself to those involved as a determination to take their worries and concerns seriously, and to provide the proper and appropriate levels of support that will be needed.

---

*Box 8.7*
*Existential choice*
Abraham Maslow (1978) observed that at every moment in our lives we have a choice between the joys of safety and the joys of growth. Far too often in the troubled and conflictual cultures of many organizations, we choose the safety option, thereby denying ourselves the possibility of development and growth, but also preventing our skills and qualities from having a greater impact on the organization itself.

---

It is the role of managers and leaders to create the nourishing and conducive conditions for change so that the choices that individuals will make will be for growth, challenge and achievement, and not a retreat into the familiar and comfortable. We can no longer afford the desperate and somewhat blind drive through the danger zones that we have traditionally taken, we need a diversion which spends appropriate time in preparation zones where appropriate attention can be given to the conceptual, emotional, aspirational and practical changes involved. We like to have control over our journeys in life, and we also like to choose our own method of transport. We all get there in the end, ready and prepared for what is to come.

Effective leadership is the process of helping our colleagues to manage change in their lives in ways that acknowledge the challenges involved, provide the support required and which do justice to their own potential.

---

*Box 8.8*
*Motivation and change*
(Roszak, 1995)
What do people need, what do they fear, what do they want? What makes them do what they do: reason or passion, altruism or selfishness? Above all, what do they love? The question of motivation sets the tone and shapes the tactics. Start from the assumption that people are greedy brutes, and the tone of all you say will be one of contempt. Assume that people are self destructively stupid, and your tactics are apt to become overbearing at best, dictatorial at worst . . . Call someone's entire life into question and what you are apt to produce is defensive rigidity.

---

Roszak further notes that the shame we sometimes feel when we are worried about our capacities to bring about personal change can quickly slide into resentment if that sense of shame is used by managers as a stick to beat us with. It is elementary psychology, he suggests, that those who wish to bring about change in others should not begin by villifying them, or by confronting them with a task that appears impossible.

> - Reflect on significant change projects you have been involved in. How did you manage the four types of adaptation referred to in this section?
> - How do you respond to expressions of resistance when colleagues are struggling with their fears and concerns about proposed changes to their ways of working?
> - How is an understanding of the psychological processes involved in change reflected in your own leadership style?

## Professional learning

Schools are in the learning business. As a profession, however, we have not always been as attentive to the processes of our own learning as we have to those of the pupils we teach. In a learning school, the professional development of the staff assumes equal importance to that of pupils. We have tended to find an emphasis on professional knowledge and skill in programmes of in-service teacher education. Future development will involve a shift from the outer world of behaviour, performance and appearance to a focus on the inner world of thoughts, feelings and experiences. Professional capability needs to be as concerned with human insight and understanding as it has traditionally been with pupil behaviour and attainment.

The skills and qualities of our profession have been considerably underestimated. Teaching has been regarded as a job almost anyone could do, given sufficient subject knowledge, and it is not that many years ago that subject graduates were first required to undergo professional training before taking up a teaching post.

It is useful to approach the skills and qualities involved in teaching from a management perspective and attempt to create a profile of the attributes needed (Figure 8.5).

Such a taxonomy places our professional capabilities firmly in the community of those concerned with management and leadership. Indeed, the only areas where differences are significant is in the occupational skills category. Managing a classroom of learners, of whatever age is a daunting and highly demanding task. Most managers in other occupational groups at least have the advantage of

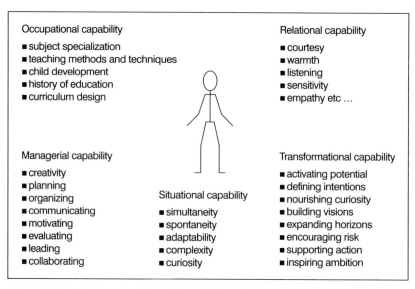

*Figure 8.5* A taxonomy of teaching skills and qualities

dealing with their clients individually, rather than in large multiple groups as teachers do.

Continuous professional learning is the means by which educators develop their practice and seek to widen their understanding of the complex process involved in human development. There is nothing simple about these processes, they have eluded categoric definition for the whole history of education and schools. There is nothing as important in the educator's professional tool kit as a driving curiosity and fascination with the process of learning. So it must be with managers, whose work focuses on the co-ordination and support of these hard-pressed educators. In management there is a long history of ignoring and resisting the needs and concerns of workers. Their inner worlds have been regarded as insignificant to their performance, and we have borne the fruits of this arrogant contempt through low productivity, poor motivation and relentless resistance to change and development.

The kinds of dynamic and adaptive professional learning necessary in the twenty-first century will require a wider curriculum than the one we have become accustomed to, with its emphasis on curriculum content and strategic design. Five particular perspectives will be significant:

- complexity consciousness
- adaptive capability
- vision-building
- tribal intelligence
- holistic reconnection.

### Complexity consciousness

For over 300 years we have slavishly followed the lead of science in viewing the world as fundamentally tidy and predictable, obeying fixed and well-understood laws. It is only very recently in the last decade or so of this century that some scientists, recognizing the harmful and limiting effects of this simplistic approach, have become interested in the more messy, unpredictable and complicated aspects of the planetary system. Initially coining the phrase *non-linear dynamics* to describe this new discipline, they are attempting to confront the disturbing fact that the whole really can be greater than the sum of its parts, and that the answers to life's most pressing questions can be answered within a framework of mechanistic principles and tidy theories. Complexity theory and chaos theory are becoming useful theoretical alternatives to traditional approaches, offering new insights into the most beguiling of human concerns such as the behaviour of individuals, the patterns present in human organizations and the intricacies of learning.

Recognizing that the real world consists not of an elegant arrangement of clearly definable and separated parts, these complexity theorists have come to appreciate that each of the variables in a complex system are arranged in an intricate web of relationships, connecting with each other in a variety of ways.

---

*Box 8.9*
*Complexity*
(Waldrup, 1992)
Complex systems have a number of significant features:

- They consist of a great many independent agents interacting with each other in a great many ways.
- The very richness of these interactions allows the system as a whole to undergo *spontaneous self-organization*.
- Complex self-organizing systems are adaptive, in that they don't passively respond to events, they actively try to turn whatever happens to their advantage.
- Adaptive, self-organizing systems possess a kind of dynamism that makes them qualitatively different from static objects such as computer chips or snowflakes, which are merely complicated.

---

Waldrup further suggests that complex systems, like the schools we are concerned with, have somehow acquired the ability to bring order and chaos into a special kind of balance often called *the edge of chaos*, where the components of a system never quite lock into place, and yet never quite dissolve into turbulence. The edge of chaos is the constantly shifting battle zone between stagnation and anarchy, and is the one place where a complex system can be spontaneous, adaptive and alive.

In the best human organizations there seems to be an instinctive understanding of this problem, where controls and regulations are neither too rigid nor too relaxed, thus creating optimum conditions for dynamic spontaneity upon which so much of human endeavour depends. As managers we need to develop the consciousness which will allow us to work comfortably within the uncertainties and inconsistencies of this complexity. We must stop the desire always to want orderliness and certainty. It is both a new way of thinking and a new way of behaving.

Complexity consciousness is particularly relevant to the management of human affairs, recognizing that with the infinite network of variables present in any school, there can never be simple solutions, easy options or straightforward strategies. Complexity consciousness involves a determination to strive for the insights and understandings that underlie the schooling process, and to recognize that outcomes do not just happen – they are the product of many variables entering into a set of relationships, becoming intensified and magnified by yet more events and incidents in the volatile system.

## Adaptive capability

The learning organization will be one that transcends the traditional organizational assumptions about human potential. It will recognize that people themselves are the active force in the pursuing of organizational aims, with a wealth of energy, skill and talent available for realizing them. These vital capabilities will need to be harnessed and focused as never before in the adaptive process. Leaders will play a significant part in the development of each individual's adaptive development, helping them to approach their working life from a creative and open-ended perspective, rather than from narrow, predetermined and a restrictive viewpoint. Adaptive capability embodies the process of continuous clarification of what is important. It is about learning how to see our complex reality more clearly, as an ally and not as an enemy.

Adaptive capability stems from a dynamic relationship between vision – a clear picture of a desired future, and purpose – a specific driving force towards it. This can create structural tensions between those forces drawing individuals towards their goals, and those forces anchoring them to traditional beliefs and values. Adaptive capability creates a relentless willingness to root out the ways in which we limit or deceive ourselves from seeing what really is.

## Imaginative flexibility

The evolutionary crisis requires us to abandon our reliance on linear and vertical thinking as the chief sources of mental activity. Creativity and the greater use of imagination and intuition will need to balance our traditional obsession with rationality and logic. Increasing reliance will need to be placed on the use of reflection and enquiry skills, particularly those that enable us to challenge the assumptions that hinder and inhibit the building of creative scenarios for change. Far from being private and personal possessions, our minds will need to be more open to enquiry and comment from our colleagues so that we can avoid what Chris Argyris (1982) calls *skilled incompetence* – that capacity to protect ourselves from the pain and threat posed by new learning situations.

---

Box 8.10
Imaginization
(Morgan, 1993)
Imaginization is a way of thinking. It's a way of organizing. It's a key managerial skill. It provides a way of helping people understand and develop their creative potential. It offers a means of finding innovative solutions to difficult problems . . . It provides a means of empowering people to trust themselves and find new roles in a world characterized by flux and change.

Imaginization offers a means whereby people in everyday situations can explore and challenge taken for granted assumptions while opening new avenues for understanding and action. I believe that it offers an approach to organization and management that demystifies the process of theory building and shows how it is possible for everyone to become their own theorists, developing penetrating insights about the organization in which they work and their roles within them.

---

The skills of imaginative flexibility will grow from the approaches to professional learning outlined earlier in this chapter. Such flexibility, drawing together the enormous stock of imagination contained within a school is a key pathway to the future.

## Vision-building

The learning organization is one that engages in the active process of envisioning – a collaborative activity to design and describe the future that reflects the collective aims and aspirations of those making up the organization. In this sense vision needs to be seen as a calling rather than simply a good idea. Shared vision can uplift people's aspirations, create sparks of excitement, compel experimentation and risk taking and increase the courage to succeed. Shared vision can never be *official*, it needs both to bubble up the organization as well as to filter down, connecting personal visions in an elaborate tracery of ambition and purpose. Vision is not to be seen as a solution to problems, but rather a driving force for the process of co-creation. It is the central element of leadership work, relentless and never ending. It involves constant attention to three key questions:

1 What does the future we are seeking to create look like?
2 Why are we pursuing this particular vision?
3 How do we behave to be consistent with the vision we are committed to?

Vital too, in this process, will be the power of our professional dreams, in which we focus our passions and commitments to the next generation. Tangible targets and behavioural objectives are necessary and useful, but not until they can become the precise and specific focus points of our bigger visions and dreams for the future.

## Tribal intelligence

Learning organizations have recognized for some time that collaboration together with a proper individualism is the key source of dynamic strength for development. An increasing tendency to tackle work through task groups and temporary teams requires attention to the processes of collaboration as well as to the work itself. If the potential of participants is to be harnessed effectively, there will need to be a focus on collective learning, similar to the traditional approaches to work inherent in tribal communities where communal survival is the key imperative. There will need to be an enhanced capacity to use conflict creatively and to use dialogue rather than mere discussion to root out defective thinking habits and defensive routines (Box 8.11).

We need to redeem this tribal intelligence as the chief source for adaptation and improvement. It will need to become a way of life.

## Holistic reconnection

This is the overarching discipline for seeing wholes, patterns and relationships. It looks for the structures that underlie complex situations and involves a shift of mind and thinking – from seeing parts to seeing wholes; from seeing people as helpless victims of change to seeing them as active participants in adaptation and development; and from reacting to the present to creating the future.

In the management of schools it means that our task is to reconnect schooling to living, and learning to life. For too long education has

Box 8.11
*Dialogue*
(Senge, 1990)
Dialogue is the capacity of colleagues to suspend traditional assumptions and to enter into a genuine *thinking together* process.

To the Greeks *dia-logos* meant a free flowing of meaning through a group, allowing the group to discover insights not attainable individually. Interestingly, the practice of dialogue has been preserved in many primitive cultures, such as that of the American Indian, but it has almost completely lost to modern society.

The discipline of dialogue involves learning to recognize the patterns of interactions in teams that undermine learning. The patterns of defensiveness are often deeply ingrained in how a team operates. If unrecognized they will undermine learning. If recognized they can actually accelerate learning.

Team learning is vital because teams, not individuals, are the fundamental learning unit in modern organizations. Unless teams can learn, the organization cannot learn.

been seen as something that is separate from living, something you have to do in a specific time and in a specific place in order to qualify for adulthood and work. This painful fragmenting of life's essential oneness cannot be the answer to the future. Schools must become places where life is lived to the full, both by the pupils and their teachers. They must be places where dreams are nourished, visions built, doors opened and opportunities empowered. For the first time in our history our schools will be concerned less with individual success and more with collaborative survival.

These five perspectives will converge to create powerful and effective learning organizations. While developing separately, each will prove critical to the other's success, just as in any effective ensemble. Each provides a vital dimension in building organizations that can truly learn and enhance their capacity to realize their highest aspirations. Success and achievement will depend upon certain characteristics being developed:

1 A shift from an instrumental to a sacred attitude to work.
2 A community where mutual support replaces individual exploitation.
3 A covenant between the individual and the organization as opposed to a contract.

The learning organization is one that is geared to change and determined to develop and refine its capacities to move into the future with confidence, curiosity and commitment.

Professional learning in the future will need to have two key directional thrusts. The first will be into the workings of human growth and development, both in terms of pupils and their learning, but also in terms of staff and their professionalism. Through the processes of action research, collaborative enquiry and reflective practice we must strive to gain deep insights into the intricate and sometimes fragile processes involved in personal development. The second will be towards the future and the building of a skilful tendency to spot trends, make connections and anticipate change. It is the opposite of what we have tended to use history for. What we now need is foresight – the capacity to look ahead and see the emerging patterns so rapidly approaching us.

- Consider the taxonomy of professional skills and qualities (Figure 8.5). How might such a classification help in the professional development of teachers?
- Review the five perspectives outlined. How do you respond to each of these?
- What do you see as the most significant factors affecting professional development in the future?

# 9 Education and the future

> There remains an underlying mystery about the process of managing. What takes place is still beyond our control, and beyond our awareness. It is as though it has a life of its own which is always beyond our grasp. Techniques make take us to the doors of this mystery, but to enter more fully into the creative process, a new level of self understanding is required. We need to learn how to trust and engage this hidden inner dimension.
> (Evans and Russell, 1990)

## Introduction

The future direction of the education service in this country will be affected by the decisions taken by politicians, but it will be determined by those who run our schools. This book has outlined the highly complex and demanding challenges that face our profession in the years to come, and explored some of the issues that are likely to affect them. In this final chapter it is to these people that we now turn, to consider the particular combination of skills, qualities, values and capabilities that they will need in the demanding times ahead.

This chapter will:

- offer a model of professional capabilities for the future managers of our schools
- outline the elements that make up the categories of this model
- present a series of reflective activities designed to support professional development.

## New millennium educators

Over the past decade or so we have witnessed the development of new approaches to the management of complexity and confusion, and the emergence of new combinations of human qualities among those who are determined to meet the future with optimism and imagination. As the paradigm shift accelerates, new people will emerge, with fresh ideas, new skills and qualities and new visions of what is possible. Many of whom David Hicks (1994) describes as *new Utopians* are already working in the system, striving to make our schools the nourishing foundation for a more humanistic, equal and optimistic world. Emerging from a variety of perspectives is a view of what these new millennium educators will be like. What characterizes them is a determination to rise above orthodoxy and convention in the pursuit of what they really believe in. What unites them is the fact that they present a new face to the world, a pattern which has not been seen before, except perhaps in rare individuals. Such a pattern is set out in Figure 9.1.

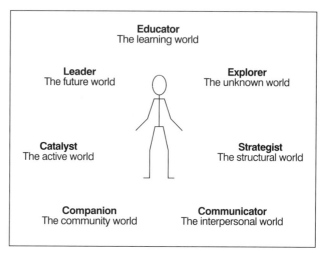

*Figure 9.1*   New millennium educators

What Figure 9.1 illustrates is a complex pattern of interconnecting worlds in which the life of a school is played out. All of us are involved in each of these worlds, but not in any logical or systematic way. The worlds interweave one with another, and at any one time we are likely to find ourselves in the intersections of any number of them. While there is an inherent untidiness and unpredictability in the threads we weave through these various worlds, there is a sense of inevitability about the complexity inherent in them. But this is what life is like. We cannot order it and control it to a strict design, nor can we manage it easily to our own purposes. Each of us is but one small yet significant part in an inordinate cluster of variables, constantly forming and reforming connections within and across the different worlds. The management of such complexity calls for considerable capability, courage and confidence, it is not for the faint hearted, the easily disappointed or the lovers of a quiet life.

The psychologist and writer Sam Keen (1991) notes a set of qualities in the people he describes as *pathfinders*: 'In every society, there are extraordinary men and women who, for a variety of reasons, stand outside the social consensus, shatter the norms, and challenge the status quo.'

In his book *The Reinvention of Work*, Matthew Fox (1994) notes that if there is no bliss in our work, no passion, no ecstasy – then we have not yet found our work. We have not experienced that sense of awakening that sets pathfinders on their way. We may have a job, but we do not have work. New millennium educators certainly have work to do, and perhaps the secret lies in our capacity to move with ease and confidence through the seven worlds outlined in Figure 9.1.

## Educator: the learning world

The word 'educator' carries a more profound and comprehensive meaning than 'teacher' to describe the work we will need to do in the future. If we need new concepts and new practices, then we will need new terms and new definitions. As managers of the learning world our work will involve a more comprehensive range of activities than have traditionally been associated with teaching, particularly by those outside the system. Among important capabilities will be:

- *Future focus*: a deep commitment to the future and a belief in the power of future generations to improve the world.
- *Belief in potential*: a powerful belief in the potential of the young to learn effectively and acquire the knowledge, skills and quality they will need to manage their lives successfully.
- *Fascination with learning*: an unfailing fascination with the complex processes of learning, development and growth.
- *Listening to experience*: a determination to listen to the experiences of pupils, and to engage with them in realizing their own hopes and aspirations for the future.
- *Being a learner*: a capacity to see ourselves as learners first and teachers second; a recognition that the pursuit of learning is a partnership of endeavour between pupils and their teachers.

**Activity 9.1**

| Capability | Specific actions I will take to develop this capability in my work. |
|---|---|
| Focus on the future | |
| Belief in potential | |
| Fascination with learning | |
| Listen to experience | |
| Be a learner first | |

## Explorer: the unknown world

New millennium educators have a pioneering spirit about them, relishing the challenges of the unknown. They appreciate that the discoveries of the past are sources of strength, but are insufficient in themselves to provide the answers to the future. Alternative directions will need to be found, and new pathways discovered. Those who practise management will have to discover a fresh sense of adventure, a new spirit of enquiry in their relentless search for ideas and possibilities. Among the explorer's chief capabilities will be:

- *Embracing change*: a predisposition to working with continuous change in a world characterized by turbulence, uncertainty and confusion.
- *Awe and wonder*: a capacity to attend to the diverse phenomena of working life with a sense of awe and wonder, as if seeing things for the first time.
- *Curiosity*: a driving curiosity about the complexities of human behaviour and why people behave as they do.
- *Living with fear*: recognizing that there are no simple solutions in management and no quick fixes; understanding that making journeys into the unknown involves the confronting of fears – fear of self, fear of others, fear of loss, fear of embarrassment, fear of failure.
- *Feeling lost*: being comfortable when not knowing where we are and what lies ahead, which way to turn and which option will work best.
- *Courage*: to go where others, as well as ourselves, fear to tread; to confront difficulties, to face up to realities and sometimes to contemplate the inconceivable.

**Activity 9.2**

| Capability | Specific actions I will take to develop this capability in my work. |
|---|---|
| Embracing change | |
| Awe and wonder | |
| Curiosity | |
| Living with fear | |
| Feeling lost | |
| Courage | |

# Strategist: the structural world

While the structural world is recognizable territory to most managers, strategic work in the years ahead will often be conducted in landscapes which are less familiar. The structures and systems we design for a fast-changing world will require an endemic flexibility, making them capable of adapting to new pressures and stresses, as and when they arise. Developing and maintaining a sense of strategic direction will not be easy in the messy blending of these different worlds, but will be a vital component of the effective school. Key factors in our strategic work will be:

- *Process*: realizing that how we do things is often more important than what we do; strategy is about the journey as well as the destination.
- *Choice*: appreciating that we are in charge of our own destinies and that we have more freedoms of choice than we sometimes realize – what we think, how we feel, what we believe, how we behave, what we fear, what we imagine, what our dreams and aspirations are, where we place our allegiances and where we direct our energy.
- *Interdependence*: understanding the infinite variety of forces, factors, causes and consequences at work within the daily life of a school, and recognizing the powerful relationships of interdependence that operate between them.
- *Vision*: building powerful visions that synthesize and crystallize the collected hopes and aspirations of all those who are involved in the school.
- *Policy*: generating a powerful shared commitment to agreed courses of action.
- *Navigating*: finding ways through stumbling blocks and obstacles, planning alternative routes and bringing projects back on course.
- *Arriving*: knowing when a job is done, recognizing successes and achievements, drawing things to a conclusion.

**Activity 9.3**

| Capability | Specific actions I will take to develop this capability in my work. |
|---|---|
| Process | |
| Choice | |
| Interdependence | |
| Vision | |
| Policy | |
| Navigating | |
| Arriving | |

# Communicator: the interpersonal world

The schooling process is intensely interactive. Despite grand visions, clear policies and specific plans, the essential business of a school is conducted through an endless sequence of interactions and encounters. Some of these are planned and intentional, but perhaps most are incidental – created in the spontaneity of the moment out of need, circumstances or location.

Frequently, these incidental encounters are interruptions to other interactions or activities, and we temporarily disengage to give them our attention. It is often in these unexpected encounters that we do our best work – dealing with difficulties, supporting people, making agreements, resolving problems, clarifying action and keeping things moving. We are operating in a process world which straddles all the others outlined in this chapter – moving through an intricate web of highly charged and dynamic signs, signals, messages, comments, questions, initiatives, demands, requests and responses.

There is also enormous potential in these encounters for disagreements, misunderstandings, disputes, tensions, hurt feelings, misplaced trust, betrayal and conflict. Much will depend upon our skills as communicators and how we behave in these snatched moments that so characterize a typical day at school. With increased turbulence, pressure and stress, the quality of these interactions will become ever more important, and success will very much depend upon how we manage ourselves in the interpersonal world. Some of the key factors which will determine our capability are:

- *Self-awareness*; striving to keep in accurate touch with our own patterns of thoughts, feelings and behaviours, and the effects these have on those we interact with.
- *Authenticity*; a deep concern to communicate what we are thinking and feeling, without deceit, dissembling and concealment.
- *Care*; a genuine desire to reach out to others and to be of help, sharing ourselves in a gentle non-do-gooding way.
- *Receptivity*; being open to approaches from others, however trivial and insignificant they may seem from an objective point of view.
- *Understanding*; seeking first to understand others before we ourselves seek to be understood by them.
- *Empathy*; listening with deep interest and sensitivity to the experiences of others and conveying our acceptance and sensing of that experience back to them.
- *Trust*; striving to build relationships of openness, warmth and mutual trust in which there are no lies and hidden agendas.

**Activity 9.4**

| Capability | Specific actions I will take to develop this capability in my work. |
|---|---|
| Self awareness | |
| Authenticity | |
| Care | |
| Receptivity | |
| Understanding | |
| Empathy | |
| Trust | |

# Companion: the community world

There seems to be a desire deep within us to share our lives with others, and the capacity to stick together in both joy and adversity has been a characteristic of social activity throughout the ages. It is sad, therefore, to find how little this need has been reflected in the management of our organizations. The tendency for those who run organizations to exploit our knowledge and skill, and to ignore our yearnings for social cohesion and a sense of community, has resulted in the separation of our mission in life – our work, from our need for economic survival – our job.

New understandings of the nature and importance of organizational culture are leading to new approaches in the ways we organize the workplace and treat those who operate within it. Letting go of the harmful traditions upon which much management practice has been built will be a continuing need in the years ahead. Those who seek, and achieve, senior management positions in schools should see themselves more as companions in a shared enterprise, than supervisors of inferior levels of activity.

Freed from connotations of rigidly disciplined regimes, compulsory attendance and uniform social order, schools have the potential to become the most exciting and enterprising communities in society. Indeed, inspections are finding a significant relationship between academic achievement and a sense of community within the school. Schools have an enormous potential to lead the paradigm shift towards new types of community-focused organizations.

In developing our capabilities in this community world some key factors will be:

- *Culture*: a deep understanding of the powerful effects organizational culture can have on those involved, and a determination to focus deliberately on culture development in the strategic work of the school.
- *Community*: recognizing the deep yearnings we all have for community, and working tirelessly to build close and intimate relationships in groups, committees and teams.
- *Support*: helping others to appreciate that although they may feel lonely, they are not alone, working to provide networks of support as part of the significant trend towards new types of friendships, partnerships, alliances and communities.
- *Affiliation*: building a culture in which a powerful sense of belonging and identification is experienced by all.
- *Encouragement*: recognizing that everyone in a school – pupils and teachers alike – face significant challenges, and creating a climate of encouragement in which our deep potentialities and best efforts can be released.

- *Challenge*: a sense of working in the world of big ideas and significant opportunities, and creating conditions in which we all aim high, take risks and learn from experience.
- *Conviviality*: creating the capacity for shared enjoyment, fun, delight and achievement.
- *Celebration*: identifying successes, and pausing to acknowledge and celebrate the achievements of individuals and groups.

**Activity 9.5**

| Capability | Specific actions I will take to develop this capability in my work. |
|---|---|
| Culture | |
| Community | |
| Support | |
| Affiliation | |
| Encouragement | |
| Challenge | |
| Conviviality | |
| Celebration | |

## Catalyst: the active world

Perhaps the most fascinating aspect of management and organizational work is the impact that personal behaviour can have on our aspirations, commitments and energy. Leadership is the art of behaving in ways that enhance and increase the capabilities and determinations of those we work with, helping them towards achievements they may not have been able to reach on their own.

This complex and elusive phenomenon can be described as a catalytic process – a capacity to bring about change in others without undergoing change ourselves. This traditional scientific definition only hints at the many factors involved in the process and we must note that in human relationships the change can be for better or for worse. When it empowers potential in the interests of the organization then it is good leadership; when it crushes or inhibits that potential then it is bad leadership.

This catalytic quality can also be described as a connecting energy flowing between people, enhancing capability and sometimes inspiring significant personal change and development. This process is central to our dual role in school – educator and manager. Some of its essential ingredients are:

- *Inner worlds*: a capacity to recognize the vital importance of the inner dimension of human experience and to share our own inner world with others.
- *Attentiveness*: the power to give others our warm, sensitive and undivided attention, conveying a deep interest in their experiences and concerns.
- *Intuition*: a sort of whole-brain knowing, based on immediacy, hunches, urges and gut reactions.
- *Responsiveness*: a process of giving back or responding to others, combined with a realization that we can make a difference in the world, and that our contributions are significant to the wider scheme of things.
- *Fun and joy*: taking life seriously but expressing delight and satisfaction in doing so; helping others to rise out of the belief that fun and serious endeavour are incompatible.
- *Belief in others*: demonstrating a powerful belief in others and their undoubted capacity to be more successful than they currently are.

**Activity 9.6**

| Capability | Specific actions I will take to develop this capability in my work. |
|---|---|
| Inner worlds | |
| Attentiveness | |
| Intuition | |
| Responsiveness | |
| Fun and joy | |
| Belief in others | |

## Leader: the future world

Leadership is by definition concerned with the future. It is about where we want to be, rather than with where we are now. It is a capacity to make dreams come true that really singles out leaders, whatever the level of activity involved. Teaching is essentially a leadership process – leading learners to future states of knowing and capability. Leadership is always practised in the common good, never to serve only self-interest and personal ambition.

The shift from leadership styles based on command and control to ones demonstrated through encouragement and support is well under way. The factors that create effective leadership are a tantalizing combination of predispositions, values, assumptions, determinations, behaviours and situations. We shall probably never crack this mysterious code, but some of the ingredients we will need in our leadership work are:

- *Sense of self:* realizing that our lives have a mission and that we have the capability and drive to reach beyond traditionally imposed limitations.
- *Freedom:* knowing that we can operate beyond apparent restrictions and inhibitions and disengage from the cultural trance which makes us obedient to the behaviours that others have designed for us, because they are best for them.
- *Vocation:* having a sense of direction in our work that is greater than a goal, and making our way in life towards something that we really want to do.
- *Being out in front:* being prepared to take the lead, to be out in front facing the difficulties and finding the pathways for others to follow.
- *Holding the vision:* being the standard bearer for a communal enterprise.
- *Service:* an unstinting dedication to the cause, and a commitment to harness the efforts of all in its service.

**Activity 9.7**

| Capability | Specific actions I will take to develop this capability in my work. |
|---|---|
| Sense of self | |
| Freedom | |
| Vocation | |
| Being out in front | |
| Holding the vision | |
| Service | |

The evolutionary crisis is an exciting context in which to be managing, drawing as it does on our deepest reserves of creativity and imagination. At the very heart of the transformational process is learning, and we need to see this innate capacity in a new light, recognizing it as the key adaptive resource we have. In the past, the emphasis was on accumulation, gathering information and knowledge almost for its own sake. In the future it will be ingenuity, vision, imagination and enterprise that will characterize the well educated, for as Eric Hoffer (1985) says: 'In a time of drastic change it is the learners who inherit the future, the learned find themselves equipped to live in a world that no longer exists.'

# Bibliography

Anthony, P. (1994). *Managing Culture*. Buckingham: Open University Press.

Argyris, C. (1960). *Integrating the Individual and the Organization*. New York: John Wiley.

Argyris, C. (1973). Personality and organization theory revisited. *Administrative Science Quarterly*, **18**, 131–167.

Argyris, C. (1982). *Reasoning, Learning and Action: Individual and Organizational*. San Francisco: Jossey Bass.

Bennis, W. (1989). *Becoming A Leader*. London: Hutchinson Business Books.

Boot, J., Lawrence, J. and Morris, J. (eds) (1994). *Managing the Unknown by Creating New Futures*. London: McGraw-Hill.

Capra, F. (1996). *The Web of Life*. London: Harper Collins.

Cleveland, H. (1985). Control: the twilight of hierarchy. *New Management*, **3** (2), 14–18.

Egan, G. (1977). *You and Me*. Belmont, California: Brooks/Cole.

Elliott, J. (1981). Action research; framework for self evaluation in schools. TIQL working paper 1, mimeo. Cambridge: Cambridge Institute of Education.

Evans, R. and Russell, P. (1990). *The Creative Manager*. London: Unwin.

Ferguson, M. (1982). *The Aquarian Conspiracy*. London: Granada.

Fox, M. (1994). *The Reinvention of Work*. San Francisco: Harper.

Freire, P. (1976). *Education: The Practice of Freedom*. London: Writers and Readers Co-operative.

Fullan, M. and Hargreaves, A. (1992). *What's Worth Fighting for in your School*. Milton Keynes: Open University Press.

Gardner, H. (1993). *Multiple Intelligences*. New York: Basic Books.

Garratt, B. (1987). *The Learning Organization*. London: Fontana/Collins.

Gibson, R. (1997). *Rethinking the Future*. London: Nicholas Brearly.

Hackman, J. R. and Lawler, E. E. (1971). Employee reactions to job characteristics. *Journal of Applied Psychology*, **55**, 259–286.

Hampden-Turner, C. (1990). *Corporate Culture*. London: Hutchinson.

Handy, C. (1976). *Understanding Organizations*. London: Penguin.

Handy, C. (1989). *The Age of Unreason*. London: Business Books.

Handy, C. and Aitken, R. (1986). *Understanding Schools as Organizations*. London: Penguin.

Heisenberg, W. (1962). *Physics and Philosophy*. New York: Harper and Row.

Heisenberg, W. (1971). *Physics and Beyond*. New York: Harper and Row.

Hicks, D. (1994). *Preparing for the Future: Notes and Queries for Concerned Educators*. London: Adamantine Press.

Hicks, D. and Gwynne, M. A. (1994). *Cultural Anthropology*. London: Harper Collins.

Hicks, D. and Holden, C. (1995). *Visions of the Future: Why We Need to Teach for Tomorrow*. London: Trentham Books.

Hoffer, E. (1985). In *Vanguard Management*. (O'Toole, J., ed.) New York: Doubleday.

Howe, D. (1993). *On Being a Client: Understanding the Processes of Counselling and Psychotherapy*. London: Sage.

Johnson, G. and Scholes, K. (1989). *Exploring Corporate Strategy*. Hemel Hempstead: Prentice Hall.

Keen, S. (1994). *Fire in the Belly*. New York: Bantam.

Kennedy, C. (1991). *Guide to the Management Gurus*. London: Business Books.

Kinsman, F. (1983). *The New Agenda*. London: Spencer Stuart and Associates.

Kinsman, F. (1990). *Millennium: Towards Tomorrow's Society*. London: W. H. Allen.

Kreuger, D. W. (1992). *Emotional Business*. San Marcos, California: Avant Books.

Krok, R. (1977). *Grinding it Out: The Making of McDonalds*. New York: Berkley.

Laing. R. D. (1967). *The Politics of Experience*. London: Penguin.

Lewin, K. (1936). *Principles of Topological Psychology*. New York: McGraw-Hill.

Lewin, R. (1995). *Complexity Life at the Edge of Chaos*. London: Phoenix.

Macy, J. (1995). Working through environmental despair. In *Ecopsychology* (Roszak, T., Gomes, M. and Kanner, A., eds) pp. 240–259. San Francisco: Sierra Books.

Marshall, J. (1994). Re-visioning organizations by developing female values. In *Managing the Unknown By Creating New Futures*. (Boot, J., Lawrence, J. and Morris, J., eds) London: McGraw-Hill.

Maslow, A. (1978). *The Farther Reaches of Human Nature*. London: Penguin.

Mintzberg, H. (1973). *The Nature of Managerial Work*. New York: Harper and Row.

Morgan, G. (1986). *Images of Organization*. London: Sage.

Morgan, G. (1993). *Imaginization*. London: Sage.

Murgatroyd, S. and Morgan, C. (1993). *Total Quality Management and the School*. Buckingham: Open University Press.

Nicholson, J. (1992). *How Do You Manage?* London: BBC Books.

Peck, M. S. (1985). *The Road Less Travelled*. London: Rider.

Pedler, M., Burgoyne, J. and Boydell, T. (1991). *The Learning Company*. London: McGraw-Hill.

Peters, T. (1988). *Thriving on Chaos*. London: Macmillan.

Peters, T. (1992). *Liberation Management*. London: Macmillan.

Peters, T. and Waterman, R. (1982). *In Search of Excellence*. New York: Harper and Row.

Pirsig, R. (1978). *Zen and the Art of Motorcycle Maintenance*. London: Corgi.

Postman, N. (1997). *The End of Education: Redefining the Value of School*. (In press).

Prigogine, I. (1979). *From Being to Becoming*. San Francisco: W. H. Freeman.

Pugh, D. S. and Hickson, D. J. (1989). *Writers on Organizations*. London: Penguin.

Revans, R. (1980). *Action Learning*. London: Blond and Briggs.

Rilke, R. M. (1975). *Rilke on Love and Other Difficulties*. New York: W. W. Norton.

Rogers, C. (1980). *On Personal Power*. London: Constable.

Roszak, T. (1981). *Person/Planet*. London: Granada.

Roszak, T. (1995). Where psyche meets Gaia. In *Ecopsychology* (Roszak, T., Gomes, M. and Kanner, A., eds) pp. 1–17, San Francisco: Sierra Books.

Rowan, J. (1992). *Breakthroughs and Integration in Psychotherapy*. London: Whurr.

Satir, V. (1982). *Peoplemaking*. Palo Alto, California: Souvenir Press.

Schon, D. (1983). *The Reflective Practitioner*. London: Basic Books.

Senge, P. (1990). *The Fifth Discipline*. London: Century Business.

Smail, D. (1987). *Taking Care*. London: J. M. Dent & Sons.

Szent-Gyoergyi, A. (1974). Drive in living matter to perfect itself. *Synthesis*. Spring.

Talbot, M. (1996). *The Holographic Universe*. London: Harper Collins.

Toffler, A. (1971). *Future Shock*. London: Pan.

Toffler, A. (1990). *Powershift: Knowledge, Wealth and Violence at the Edge of the 21st Century*. New York: Bantam Books.

Waldrup. M. (1992). *Complexity*. New York: Simon and Schuster.

Walford, R. (1981). Language, ideologies and teaching geography. In *Signposts in Teaching Geography* (Walford, R., ed.), London: Longman.

Webb, G. (1996). *Understanding Staff Development*. Buckingham: Open University Press.

Whitaker, P. (1993). *Practical Communication Skills in Schools*. Harlow: Longman.

Whitaker, P. (1995). *Managing to Learn*. London: Cassell.

Whitaker, P. (1997). *Primary Schools and the Future*. Buckingham: Open University Press.

# Index